Creating
Standards-Based
Integrated
Curriculum

Second Edition

Creating
Standards-Based
Integrated
Curriculum

Aligning Curriculum, Content, Assessment, and Instruction

Susan M. Drake

Second Edition

CORWIN PRESS
A SAGE Publications Company
Thousand Oaks, CA 91320

For information:

Corwin Press
A Sage Publications Company
2455 Teller Road
Thousand Oaks, California 91320
www.corwinpress.com

Sage Publications Ltd
1 Oliver's Yard
55 City Road
London EC1Y 1SP
United Kingdom

Sage Publications India Pvt. Ltd.
B-42, Panchsheel Enclave
Post Box 4109
New Delhi 110 017 India

Printed in the United States of America on acid-free paper

Library of Congress Cataloging-in-Publication Data

Drake, Susan M., 1944-
Creating standards-based integrated curriculum : aligning curriculum, content, assessment, and instruction / Susan M. Drake.—2nd ed.
    p. cm.
Includes bibliographical references and index.
Previously published under title: Creating integrated curriculum.
ISBN-13: 978-1-4129-1505-2 (cloth)
ISBN-13: 978-1-4129-1506-9 (pbk.)
    1. Interdisciplinary approach in education—United States. 2. Interdisciplinary approach in education—Canada. 3. Education—United States—Curricula.
4. Education—Canada—Curricula. 5. Education—Standards—United States.
6. Education—Standards—Canada. I. Title.
LB1570.D695 2007
375.000973—dc22

                                        2006034836

07   08   09   10   11   10   9   8   7   6   5   4   3   2

Acquisitions editor:	Faye Zucker
Editorial assistant:	Gem Rabanera
Production editor:	Sanford Robinson
Copy editor:	Julie Gwin
Typesetter:	C&M Digitals (P) Ltd.
Indexer:	Kirsten Kite
Cover designer:	Monique Hahn

Contents

List of Figures and Tables

Chapter 1

Chapter 5

Chapter 6

Chapter 7

Chapter 8

Appendix C

Preface

Recently, I was riding on the Toronto subway when I spotted an intriguing billboard. It was advertising the "Interdisciplinary University." Some examples of the ads that attracted me were the following:

> *A picture of a cigarette accompanies the text—*
> *. . . A chemist sees formaldehyde.*
> *. . . A child psychologist sees peer pressure.*
> *. . . A law student sees class action.*
>
> *A picture of Earth from space accompanies the text—*
> *. . . An historian sees war.*
> *. . . A geologist sees fossil fuels.*
> *. . . An engineer sees space stations.*
>
> *A picture of earphones accompanies the text—*
> *. . . An anthropologist sees the latest trend.*
> *. . . A behavioral scientist sees the privacy.*
> *. . . A marketer sees piracy.*
> *QUESTION EVERY ANGLE.*
> *STUDY EVERY ANGLE.*
> *RESEARCH EVERY ANGLE.*
> *WELCOME TO THE INTERDISCIPLINARY UNIVERSITY.*
>
> —York University, 2005

I was startled by this ad in my own backyard. This was not a wild, futuristic vision of education. Currently, there are thematic programs in entertainment and culture, environmental sustainability, international studies, and health research at York University, Toronto, Ontario. I was interested in the promotional material claiming that creative, interdisciplinary collaborations are considered the only way that learning can advance the human condition (York University, 2005).

I was also startled by a project at another local university. Consider the following scenario: A patient is in dire need of a complicated surgery. He lives in a remote community, and the specialist in his disease works in a large, metropolitan hospital. The patient is too sick to travel. He goes to his local hospital for the operation. Here, robotic arms are linked by space-age technology to the expert surgeon, who controls and manipulates these arms from thousands of miles away. A local surgeon assists. This scenario is a reality. Interdisciplinary project teams at the University of Western Ontario can perform complex yet minimally invasive operations, from cardiac bypass to cancer therapy. Surgeons, students, researchers in surgery, engineers, and experts in imaging, information technology, and business work together to create the conditions for these robotic surgeries. In 2005, Canadian Surgical Technologies & Advanced Robotics Centre had completed more than 600 robotic surgeries (see www.c-star.ca). The interdisciplinary teams are much more creative and innovative than a team that works simply from a disciplinary perspective.

For years, I have worked with educators to develop interdisciplinary programs. My experiences have been overwhelmingly positive. I also know many teachers are reenergized by the process. And when teachers implement these types of programs, they usually have the same positive results as others before them.

From the longitudinal Eight-Year Study (Aikin, 1942) until more recently, research continues to indicate that in interdisciplinary programs, students do as well as or better than students in traditional programs (see, for example, Curry, Samara, & Connell, 2005; Drake & Burns, 2004; Expeditionary Learning Outward Bound, 2001; Ferrero, 2006; Vars, 2001). Also, interdisciplinary approaches lead to better attendance records, fewer discipline problems, and more engaged and motivated students.

The electronic newsletter *Edutopia* often provides examples of fascinating interdisciplinary projects and research-based evidence that interdisciplinary approaches are successful (www.edutopia.org). Also, the Harvard Graduate School of Education provides an excellent e-mail newsletter with a wide variety of inspiring examples of educational innovation (http://wideworld.pz.harvard.edu).

Yet some teachers always seemed to resist. The last stronghold of their resistance always seemed to be:

I have to teach strictly in my discipline to prepare my students for the next grade (or high school, or university).

How would these teachers respond to the possibility that they are preparing students for an interdisciplinary experience at the next level? And how are educators preparing K–12 students for a future in higher education such as this?

SEEKING RIGOR AND RELEVANCE

I have always believed in making the curriculum relevant. For me, if the curriculum isn't relevant, students will not learn. If the students do not learn, there is not much point in teaching. This is a simple axiom, but it is one that I believe now as strongly as when I began teaching more than 35 years ago.

I suspect this belief in relevance is based primarily on my own experiences both as a student and as a high school teacher. I was not a student who loved school. I can remember only one teacher who really turned me on to learning. I was in Grade 5, and Mr. Griffin made Marco Polo's adventures come alive. I was actively involved in classroom activities and filled with brilliant images of the Orient dancing through my head. Perhaps that is why I longed to travel the world—to have my own adventures. But apart from this one experience, school was boring and unrewarding.

Blessed with a good memory, I could memorize what I needed to know for the tests. Thus, I passed the tests and even skipped a grade. My teachers taught a lot of things, but I did not learn what I was supposed to learn. Although I passed the tests, I quickly forgot what I had memorized and regurgitated. Today, I hesitate to play games like Trivial Pursuit because so many of the things I learned in school are gone. The knowledge that had once been so important to test and make sure I could regurgitate had disappeared as surely as if my mind was a sieve. It seems like the only things I truly remember are the things that I have needed to use in later life.

As a teacher, I was even more aware of the necessity for relevance. I was not a natural disciplinarian. To this day, young people laugh if I try to discipline them with a stern, hard voice. Instead, to capture my audience, I must make the curriculum so relevant that students want to learn. Only then can I bypass the need for strong classroom management skills. As a result, I spent hours trying to devise the most interesting lessons to capture the interest of my students. Most important, I was always trying to connect the curriculum to the students—their lives and their interests.

In hindsight, I see that I stumbled into interdisciplinary curriculum as a desperate classroom management tool. My first attempt is still vivid in my mind. I was having trouble making the Grade 10 English lesson engaging. As it happened, I taught physical education to the girls as well as English. One day, I was teaching body language as a communication tool. The girls already knew a folk dance, and I asked them to teach the dance to the boys without any words or music. Everyone got quickly involved. They had never had an English lesson quite like this one. In fact, the experience was so unique that the word somehow spread like wildfire to students sitting in other classrooms. Before the dance class was over, there were many students who had somehow left their own classrooms and were vying for a position to press their noses against the classroom door window. The girls found it extraordinarily difficult to teach the dance without being able to talk. When the boys attempted the dance with the music for the first time, we all collapsed in laughter.

Today, I still believe that students will really learn only when the curriculum is relevant to them, and this does not mean relevant because the material is on the next test or it is something they will need to know in the next grade. But now, like everyone else, I am immersed in the accountability movement. In reality, I can no longer rely on simply creating engaging learning experiences for students. They also need to meet the standards. My students might have loved to folk dance in English class, but did they really learn the intended knowledge and skills? While I hoped and believed they did, I had no real way to measure it other than my own assessments and perceptions.

The accountability movement has permeated all aspects of education. Now I search to balance relevance and accountability. I know it can be done. I have spent the last several years learning how to do it. This book is the result of that search.

HOW THIS BOOK EVOLVED

This book began as a second edition to my 1998 Corwin Press book called *Creating Integrated Curriculum: Proven Ways to Increase Student Learning*. The 1998 book offered a smorgasbord of the best in interdisciplinary curricula from the late 1980s and early 1990s. Integrated curricula were a popular response to reports such as *Turning Points* (Carnegie Corporation, 1989) in the United States and *Rights of Passage* (Hargreaves & Earl, 1990) in Canada. These reports targeted adolescents who were not motivated to learn. Essentially, there was a call for curricula that were more relevant for young people. For many, interdisciplinary curricula provided an answer.

During this period, there was a great deal of exciting work happening in classrooms across North America and many engaged students and educators involved in innovative processes. The 1998 book offered samples of the wide range of models that emerged during this time. In short, someone could use the book and sample the state of the art in interdisciplinary models without going to several different books to discover each one.

But around the mid-1990s, the climate in education changed. The pendulum swung swiftly and dramatically. Critics of education noted that students still were not achieving at desired levels. There were renewed fears that North American students would not be able to compete in the global economy. Suddenly, there was a shift from finding relevance in the curriculum to ensuring accountability in the system. How could we know when students were achieving at satisfactory levels? The answer, of course, was the development of standards and standardized tests to ensure that the standards were being addressed adequately.

It has been a bumpy road in education since that time, as educators have tried to come to terms with the accountability measures. One of the first things that disappeared with the new mandates was the interdisciplinary approach. Many of the "gurus" of the late 1980s and early 1990s declared that integrated curriculum was dead and shifted to areas deemed more appropriate to accountability efforts.

Across North America, the associations representing the disciplines created the standards—regardless of whether they were at the national, state, provincial, or regional level. The standards, given the process, were disciplinary in nature. Teachers were busy addressing the disciplinary standards (usually there were too many in each discipline) and preparing students for the large-scale tests that were disciplinary in nature. The results of these tests were important. In many jurisdictions, a teacher's reputation was affirmed or broken by the results. Funding for the school could also be affected. For most teachers, integrated curriculum was a thing of the past. Moving through the standards of each separate discipline was the order of the day. Even those who had experienced success with integrated approaches in the past had trouble seeing any light.

During this time, I never stopped believing in the power of integration as a motivating learning tool. Perhaps it was because I had the luxury of working at the university level with practicing teachers and graduate students who were taking a course in innovative curriculum or innovative assessment. Working on these graduate credit courses, the teachers enjoyed playing with new ideas without scrutiny from their district colleagues or administrators and with the added reward of a course credit. Certainly my preservice colleagues found that, for the most part, it was impossible to use interdisciplinary approaches. Some of them also insisted that integrated curriculum was dead.

Not having to account for myself in a school system, I could not understand why people could no longer integrate. I could see the same connections across the new disciplinary standards as in previous curriculum documents. Not needing to "cover the standards," I could look at the curriculum with a wide-angle lens and see the patterns across the standards in different subject areas. I held on to my beliefs and continued to teach my graduate courses. In their role as teachers, some of my students actually had to report to the administration the standards they addressed each day. They were understandably afraid to stray far from this systematic process. But they also longed for a relevant curriculum that would capture their students' engagement. Together we tackled how we could resolve this dilemma. How could we bridge accountability and relevance? How could we satisfy parents and administrators and also the students?

At first, the graduate students and practicing teachers and I played with the models in the 1998 Corwin book. We found it relatively easy to take an existing model and create a curriculum by attaching relevant standards from the new curriculum documents. It did not take much imagination and seemed to satisfy accountability mandates. But as we explored how to truly integrate the curriculum, we found that this matching process was too easy. Looking at standards and checking them off a list as met was not good enough. We began to explore how we could really understand the standards and what they demanded we teach.

We had to go back to the beginning and begin with the standards themselves. We needed to ask basic alignment questions: Was there alignment of the curriculum, content, assessment, and instructional strategies? Were we really teaching what was most important to learn? How did we know when we had successfully taught it? How could we honor the standards in a discipline and still do interdisciplinary work? How could we create relevant activities that would lead to learning the most important standards? Could we build a bridge across the disciplines built with the standards themselves?

Over time, and with a great deal of classroom experimentation, we discovered ways to integrate the curriculum that satisfied accountability mandates *and* allowed us to create curriculum that was relevant for students (Drake & Burns, 2004). Sometimes the relevance involved setting the learning in a real-life context. Sometimes it involved actually cocreating the curriculum with the students.

During the process of updating this book, I realized that I was actually creating a completely transformed and different work from the first edition. One cannot approach interdisciplinary work in a standards-based environment simply by adding standards to the late-1980s and early-1990s models (which had not previously dealt with standards). To simply match standards to activities looked good but did not really get at creating a curriculum that was deeply anchored in standards, nor did it align interdisciplinary work with assessment and instruction. Because the accountability process demanded such a different approach to curricular design, I found myself writing what seemed to be virtually a new book entirely.

Very little from the 1998 edition has been carried forward into this new edition. I did, however, describe again the three approaches to integration as a framework for understanding the range of possibilities for integration: multidisciplinary, interdisciplinary, and transdisciplinary. Also, two models offered in the 1998 book reappear here in their standards-based reincarnation—the Curry/Samara Model® and the Narrative Curriculum. Yet even though these standbys are included, this is essentially a new book.

LESSONS LEARNED

It is a strange experience to have written seven books on integrated curriculum. It may appear as if I simply write the same book over and over again, but this is far from the reality. I find myself wrestling with new ideas and ways to resolve new issues emerging from the latest policy mandates.

For each book, I have been fortunate enough to connect with or have access to some of the finest educators on the planet. Their efforts are awe inspiring, and I continually learn from them.

I always begin with a planned order for the book's content. Then I face the puzzle of how to present the parts of the material that must be understood as a whole before you can understand the parts. Inevitably, my well-intentioned and logical order turns into chaos as I come to deeper and deeper understandings of the interconnectedness of this work.

This book has been no different. It is my third venture into writing about interdisciplinary curriculum with standards in mind, but it has taken me into surprisingly new territory. It happened as I began writing Chapters 4 and 5. Suddenly, I saw bigger and bigger pictures. It meant revisiting the first three chapters to align them with my new and bigger vision. This is why most of the significant concepts in this book begin with the term *Big*.

It was also during the writing of this book that I began to understand the significance of the assessment piece. I believe now that the door to mainstream acceptance of interdisciplinary approaches is through assessment. And when one looks at interdisciplinary assessment tasks and tools, they are reassuringly familiar. It only takes a shift from the disciplinary focus to the Big Picture to see how assessment tools can work in other contexts.

I am also very aware of what is not in this book. I did not include a list of studies that support interdisciplinary work. That would have read like a long laundry list, and in my experience, such a list has done little to convert anyone. I also intended to outline the potential pitfalls of trying to do integrated approaches. This would have been accompanied by suggested strategies to avoid these pitfalls. In fact, dealing with obstacles was an important section in most of my other books.

I also did not address the differences that occur when a teacher is working alone or team teaching. These are indeed very different contexts, and each has its own problems and its own rewards. I focused on the process of standards-based design, which is similar from K through Grade 16. With a clear process, some of the obstacles, whether working alone or collaboratively, are naturally removed.

A recent experience steered me away from including obstacles as a focus. I was invited to facilitate a "conversation" on integrated approaches. It was to be an open forum with educators from a wide variety of contexts in attendance. The conversation was all about obstacles. I was shocked to find that the loudest voices blocked any discussion. Didn't I understand that they had to "cover the standards?" Didn't I know that there was not enough time for planning? Didn't I know that it was impossible to integrate math into any unit? Didn't I know that unless teachers had been trained in a discipline, they could not teach it properly? And so it went. I wondered why they had voluntarily come to this session.

I felt transported back to the days when Ontario mandated integrated curriculum for K to 9. I traveled across my province to train educators on how to integrate the curriculum. Many were resistant. I spent a lot of time and energy "watering the rocks." I was determined that all educators would come onside once they understood the advantages of interdisciplinary approaches. I learned, somewhat painfully, that rocks do not grow, no matter how much you nurture or water them. Eventually, I also learned to accept that interdisciplinary approaches are not for everyone.

Now, more than a decade later, I was meeting resistance again. I was astonished but should not have been. The resistant educators had not traveled the same path as I had for the last 16 years. My mistake in the early 1990s was not to spend all my time and energy with the excited and reenergized teachers all around me who were ready and willing to try integration. I vowed not to repeat this mistake again. No more convincing or cajoling.

This time I was rescued. Several educators in the audience were currently running very successful integrated programs. It was to these resident experts that I turned. They spoke with passion about what they were doing and the positive effects they saw with their students. They were able to counteract the resistance and provided a pragmatic answer to every question. Now, we could move on.

Thus, this book does not deal with obstacles and does not attempt to prove the worth of interdisciplinary approaches. It is for the educators who are ready and willing to embrace such an approach. As teachers work with standards and become more comfortable with them, they too see the bigger picture. They realize that to address and assess all the standards, they need to integrate the curriculum. They recognize that there is increasingly more and more information for students to manage. But they can also see that when they focus on what is most important to *know, do,* and *be,* students have a way to manage it.

THE CHAPTERS AHEAD

Each of the chapters ahead concludes with both discussion questions and suggested activities. The discussion questions center on building personal meaning for the concepts introduced in the chapters. The activities are intended to build on each other. If one engages in the activities from chapter to chapter, most of the pieces for a standards-based curriculum will be completed. By Chapter 6, the reader will be able to put the pieces together to create a standards-based interdisciplinary curriculum. It is recommended, then, that readers work with standards that are relevant to them and that they use these standards to address the activities throughout the book.

Chapter 1 explores the basics of the accountability movement. All the strategies discussed in this chapter can be used for both disciplinary and interdisciplinary work. There is a brief review of the purpose of standards and some of the challenges they pose. The quality of standards has improved over the years, and we look at how we can design a rigorous and relevant curriculum and still meet these standards. To this end, we need to engage in two-dimensional thinking—seeing both the Big Picture and the more focused disciplinary picture at the same time. From a wide-angle lens, we look at creating a Know/Do/Be Umbrella and then use the backward design process. Shifting to a zoom lens, we unpack individual standards to see what they actually require of students. Finally, we look at curriculum mapping as a precursor to integrating the curriculum.

Chapter 2 explores possible definitions for integrated curriculum. In this book, the terms *integrated* and *interdisciplinary* are used interchangeably when talking about such curriculum in general terms. Chapter 2 provides an overview of interdisciplinary education since the 1990s. Fusion, multidisciplinary, interdisciplinary, and transdisciplinary approaches to integration are described. An organizer, planning templates, and examples are offered for each approach. Finally, we look at how these approaches are affected by the standards movement—how they are similar and how they are different.

Chapter 3 explores the first question in backward mapping process. What do we want students to know, do, and be? This question is first addressed from the wide-angle lens looking at the Big Picture. When we look at the Big Picture, we ask what a student needs to learn to live successfully in society. We want students to know Big Ideas and Big Understandings. We want students to be able to demonstrate Big Skills such as research skills and communication skills. Finally, we want them to be productive citizens in a democratic society who hold and act on a positive set of values. At this point, we zoom in on the design of curriculum units. How do we identify the broader and more abstract *know, do, be* (KDB) in specific curriculum documents? A scan and cluster process is described for recognizing the *know* and the *do* in standards. The rest of the chapter offers strategies for working with the KDB at the disciplinary level.

Chapter 4 begins with exploring the concept of interdisciplinary assessment. What is interdisciplinary assessment? How do we use it? Who is responsible for teaching the interdisciplinary skills and concepts? The rest of the chapter addresses the second question of backward design. How do we know when students have learned what we want them to learn? The difference between assessment tasks and assessment tools is described. There is an example of an interdisciplinary Big Assessment task and its accompanying assessment tool. This example comes from an innovative interdisciplinary high school program in Adelaide, Australia. The Big Assessment task must be connected to the KDB Umbrella. Two examples are provided to show how teachers can make this connection.

In Chapter 5, we examine how to create the daily instructional activities. This is the last question of backward design and is intended to ensure alignment of the curriculum, standards, and assessment. The chapter begins with an exploration of how to develop Big Questions. Big Questions act as a bridge across the disciplines. There is a comparison of Big Questions and Topic Questions. A wonderful example of how to create Big Questions is offered. The connection between standards, Big Questions, and Big Understandings is also explored. In this chapter, specific ideas for creating engaging instructional activities are given. The learning principles are suggested as a fundamental consideration for planning. The focus is on generating engaging and challenging assessment tasks that are aligned with standards. This leads to engaging and challenging activities. The assessment tools connect us back to the KDB. Finally, we follow one teacher's thinking as she creates her daily activities and assessments for a unit on the Civil War. This teacher utilizes the learning principles in creating her lessons. Also, she modifies her lessons for a variety of learning styles.

Chapter 6 puts all the pieces together to design a standards-based curriculum. The process is the same for every grade level. In this sample, a Grade 4 curriculum unit on fables is featured to illustrate the principles of developing the curriculum.

Chapter 7 provides different examples of integrated curriculum. The first example comes from John Curry and John Samara from the Curriculum Project. This is a very interesting and successful approach that utilizes Bloom's taxonomy. The second example is from Marci Steele, a teacher from Pennsylvania. She has created a webquest for her students. This example shows how technology can be integrated into the curriculum. The second example is the Narrative Curriculum. This interdisciplinary approach begins with a story—usually a story with a scientific base. The lessons are generated from student questions. Finally, we look at a full-credit course outline created by a student for an independent study. This curriculum is particularly interesting because it follows the Ontario Interdisciplinary Studies Guideline (www.edu.gov.on.ca).

Chapter 8 describes the design and implementation process from beginning to end. Beyond the technical skills to design an interdisciplinary curriculum, the implementation is a complex and often challenging process. I am indebted to Tessie Torres-Dickson, a national education consultant from Tampa, Florida, for the inclusion of this chapter. Tessie has worked successfully with schools to implement her version of interdisciplinary work. In other publications, I spent a lot of words describing strategies to deal with the challenges of implementing interdisciplinary curriculum. In this book, Tessie's chapter speaks for itself. The teachers from Florida highlighted in this chapter are faced with all the challenges of a test-based culture—complete with pacer guides that dictate daily practice. Their story confirms my suspicion that, despite seemingly overriding obstacles, when there is a will, there is always a way.

Finally, in the Epilogue, I invite the reader to embark on the adventure of creating interdisciplinary standards-based curricula.

DISCUSSION QUESTIONS AND SUGGESTED ACTIVITIES

As you work through the discussions and activities, please note that you would be wisest to choose a relevant grade level and set of standards and use them for all the activities in the following chapters.

Discussion Questions

1. What is your personal experience of the relationship between accountability and relevance?

2. Does the author's personal experience with curriculum integration shed any light on your understanding?

3. Do you think the author is doing the wisest thing when she says that she will no longer "water the rocks"?

4. Think of a time when you have been involved in a change effort. Resistance is considered a normal part of change. How do you personally respond to change? In what ways have you noticed that others resist change? What factors helped to facilitate the change?

Suggested Activities

Examine the advertisements for York University. What is the most important point in these ads? Create new advertisements with a similar theme for elementary, middle, and secondary levels.

Acknowledgments

The writing of this book has been a fascinating experience. Written at a time when interdisciplinary curriculum may seem to have gone underground, I discovered that this is simply not true. Integrated approaches are everywhere—one only needs to look to find them. I am deeply grateful to the exemplary educators featured in this book who are dedicated to making school a wonderful experience for their students. I thank each and every one of them, not only for their contribution to this book but also for their tireless efforts to bridge accountability and relevance. In particular, I would like to thank Tessie Torres-Dickson, an educational consultant, for sharing her curriculum development process from beginning to end.

I was indeed fortunate to work side by side with two brilliant practicing educators. Terry Whitmell is a newly appointed vice principal in a secondary school in Ontario. She created the figures in this book. Not only is Terry a genius with technology, but, also, she understands standards-based interdisciplinary curriculum. Often, she would challenge my fuzzy thinking and then help me to clarify it. She could create the perfect graphic to represent a complex concept. Also, she provided resources from the field that were invaluable to me. I feel deeply privileged to have had the opportunity to work with Terry.

I also worked with Joanne Reid, who once taught with me at the high school level. Joanne works at the provincial level on assessment issues. Joanne acted as a critical friend as I wrote each chapter and helped to do a first edit of this book. Like Terry, she is a strong conceptual thinker who cuts through fuzziness like a knife. I could always count on her to challenge my thinking and to push me into new territory. She would never hesitate to point out my inconsistencies. I always looked forward to the next set of her comments. It was a sheer pleasure to work with Joanne.

Thanks to Spogmai Akseer and Kelly Powick-Kumar. I could always count on them to organize and keep me out of total chaos. Spogmai would run to do necessary photocopying, check Web sites, or do whatever else happened to come up. Kelly put the finishing touches on the graphics. They both helped to make the final copy look like it was supposed to.

I would also like to thank Elizabeth Rothmel, another colleague from my secondary teaching days. Elizabeth, who is now retired, once taught in the gifted program and is very familiar with integrated curriculum. With this insider knowledge, she reviewed this book and helped with the initial editing. She offered many valuable comments and corrections. I truly appreciated how quickly she returned each chapter and our ongoing conversation about what works in education. Also, I am thankful to Tony Giblin, an instructor of preservice students at Brock University. Tony was once an elementary principal, and he has a deep understanding of concept-based curriculum issues. I thank Tony for the interesting conversations over the years and appreciate his continued willingness to review my work.

I met Faye Zucker a number of years ago. She inherited me as an author since my original editor left Corwin Press and Faye replaced her. I would meet Faye at a conference and we would go for lunch to brainstorm what my next project might be. I really enjoyed those events as Faye indulged my ramblings on every idea under the kitchen sink. I thank you, Faye, for your never-ending patience, your faith that I would have another book in me, and your willingness to let it unfold as it should.

Thanks to Corwin's Sanford Robinson and Julie Gwin, as well as Gem Rabanera, who spent a great deal of time on this manuscript.

Finally, I thank my family and friends who have lived through all the ups and downs of writing this book. Thank you to Addie, Katie, Jack, and Odessa Paterson for constantly teaching me how young people learn. Thanks to Scott and Tamara Paterson for continually making life so wonderfully interesting. And thanks most of all to Michael Manley-Casimir for his patience, love, and support.

Corwin Press thanks the following reviewers for their contributions to this book:

Jane Adair, Resource Specialist, Long Beach Polytechnic High School, Long Beach, CA

Gary Babiuk, Assistant Professor, University of Minnesota–Duluth

Marion Cross, Clinical Assistant Professor, Department of Learning and Instruction, University at Buffalo, Buffalo, NY

Sue DeLay, Curriculum Resource Teacher, Oak Creek Franklin Joint School District, Oak Creek, WI

Mary Ann Kahl, Assistant Professor, National-Louis University, Milwaukee, WI

John P. Miller, Professor, Department of Curriculum, Teaching, and Learning, Ontario Institute for Studies in Education (OISE), University of Toronto

About the Author

**Susan M. Drake** is a Professor in the Graduate and Undergraduate Department of Brock University, St. Catharines, Ontario. She earned a PhD in curriculum from the University of Toronto. She has taught at all levels of education. She taught physical education and health as well as English for 18 years at the high school level. She worked on school improvement teams at the elementary level and spent one year as an elementary teacher. Also, she was a partner in a private adult education company that provided organizational development, consulting, and adult learning courses.

Today, Susan teaches curriculum and assessment courses to undergraduate, master's of education, and doctoral students and for undergraduate students who will soon be entering the teaching field. As a researcher, she seeks out educators who are involved in exemplary practices, as she believes that a good practice makes good theory. This is Susan's seventh book on the topic of curriculum integration, and she has published more than 48 articles and nine book chapters. She coauthored *Meeting Standards Through Integrated Curriculum* (2004) for ASCD with Rebecca Burns. Also, she authored *Creating Integrated Curriculum* (1998) for Corwin Press and *Planning for Integrated Curriculum: The Call to Adventure* (1993) for ASCD. She has led interdisciplinary curriculum design teams from the school to the provincial level. Susan travels extensively and has done workshops and presentations across North America and in Europe, Asia, and Africa.

ABOUT THE CONTRIBUTOR

Tessie Torres-Dickson is a National Educational Consultant working with schools and districts, specializing in the designing of standards-based interdisciplinary curriculum and instruction. Her expertise focuses on facilitating the process for curriculum development in connecting the curriculum, assessment, and instruction. She has been an educator for 25 years serving as a teacher, Florida Department of Education professional developer, consultant, keynote speaker, and presenter at national conferences, and she is currently on the board of directors for the Florida ASCD. Tessie is a past recipient of the National Science Foundation's National Presidential Awards for Excellence in Science Teaching and promotes teaching science through inquiry. Tessie may be contacted through the following information: e-mail: tessiedickson@earthlink.net; http://www.tessiedickson.com.

1

Accountability and Two-Dimensional Thinking

The goal of this book is to bridge the current need for both relevance and accountability. This first chapter explains some of the basic practices that ensure that any curriculum—be it disciplinary or interdisciplinary—follows accountability mandates. It begins with a brief discussion of accountability, the role of standards in curriculum planning, and some challenges teachers experience with standards. This follows with an exploration of the Big Picture and the Know/Do/Be Umbrella. The focus then zooms into the micro level to unpack the standards themselves. A "design-down process" is described as the template for aligning interdisciplinary work. Finally, curriculum mapping is offered as a precursor to any curriculum design and one that is useful for interdisciplinary work.

WHAT IS ACCOUNTABILITY?

Accountability is an umbrella term that generally refers to educators acting in accordance with how the public has determined they are to act and to achieve what they are expected to achieve. There are many different aspects to accountability. Darling-Hammond (2004), for example, offers the following types of accountability that have influenced educational policy:

- Political: Legislators and school board members make decisions that they answer to and must stand for election.
- Legal: Schools must operate according to school law.
- Bureaucratic: National, state (provincial), and district offices set forth rules and regulations for schools to follow.
- Market: Parents may choose what schools students go to.
- Professional: Educators are expected to acquire specialized knowledge and meet entry and professional standards of practice.

No single form of accountability stands alone. Most recently, legal and bureaucratic accountability has dominated with a focus on standardized educational procedures, prescribed curriculum and texts, and test-based accountability strategies tied to tracking.

This approach to accountability has not been particularly successful, although the general public remains largely unaware of this. Backed by convincing evidence, Darling-Hammond (2004) offers some unintended consequences for high-stakes testing, such as: the narrowing of the curriculum, the failure of grade retention to increase student success, and the encouragement of students to go into special education classes or to drop out of school.

In this book, we explore how students can meet the prescribed educational standards through an interdisciplinary curriculum that opens the curriculum rather than narrows it.

WHAT IS A STANDARDS-BASED APPROACH?

Teachers are expected to prepare students to meet the standards to ensure accountability. The taught curriculum is similar for students in the same grade across a state or province regardless of where they live. To demonstrate achievement levels, students take large-scale standardized tests. The results of these tests are intended to indicate the level of student learning.

There are many critics of these accountability policies, particularly for high-stakes, large-scale testing. When the stakes are high—funding or one's reputation—teachers can resort to ineffective teaching practices such as "teaching to the test." Students may do better on the tests by remembering material in the short term. But, in the long term, the content is easily forgotten, and there has been no real understanding of the material.

Nevertheless, accountability and standards-based approaches seem here to stay. An effective standards-based approach adopts the following premises for both disciplinary and interdisciplinary work:

- A design-down curriculum planning process is used.
- The focus is on what students will do, not what the teacher will do.
- Standards, teaching strategies, and assessment are aligned.

- It is important to decide what students should know, do, and be.
- The standards are observable and measurable.
- The assessment of standards is embedded in instructional strategies.
- Big Ideas and Big Understandings act as an umbrella for the content. They reappear in the curriculum at different levels and in different subjects (e.g., change, interdependence, conflict, objectivity, and causality).
- Big Skills (complex performance skills) reappear year after year and across subject areas (e.g., literacy, problem solving, and technological skills).
- The content is the vehicle to achieving the standards.
- The teacher is free to teach in any style as long as the standards are met.

CHALLENGES WITH STANDARDS

With each new version of curriculum documents, the standards are becoming better and better. There is a clearer consensus on what students need to know and do, and the standards themselves are articulated more clearly. At this point, the standards in most jurisdictions are somewhat different, but are also remarkably the same.

Nevertheless, some problems with standards remain:

- The quality of standards from different regions is uneven.
- There are too many standards created at too many levels of education.
- Subject areas are territorial about the importance of "their" discipline's standards.
- Not all standards are worth achieving.
- Some standards are too ambiguous.
- Some standards are too narrow and irrelevant to facilitate any deep understanding.

Often, the challenge is not in the standards themselves but in our assumptions of how to work with them. It takes thoughtfulness and patience to fully understand what a standard is asking a student to know, do, and be. Teachers often "cover the standards" in the same spirit that they cover the content. It is quite easy to check off a standard as completed, when it has not really been addressed thoroughly or it is peripheral to the learning. It is also easy to overlook any new skills that need to be taught to achieve a standard. As well, some teachers assume that once a standard is taught, it has been learned. And although all students should achieve the standard, not all students can achieve the standards in the same way at the same time.

TWO-DIMENSIONAL THINKING

A major challenge today is designing a curriculum that is both relevant and accountable. Standards have almost become a code word for accountability. Ideally, standards should actually improve student learning—not just be used to measure student learning (Darling-Hammond & Falk, 1997).

Alignment is a commonly identified strategy for improving student performance (Elmore & Rothman, 1999; Mitchell, 1998; Ohio State Department of Education, 2001). Alignment means that the standards, content, assessment, and instruction strategies make a complementary fit. Alignment is sometimes called *seamless curriculum*. Curriculum planning needs to be thoughtful, with a systematic process for continually checking to ensure that all parts are interconnected.

Teachers tend to follow the guidelines in ways that hold intact their disciplinary boundaries. This strategy may be perceived as necessary to prepare for tests or to fit in with the culture of their school or department. Staying within the boundaries of the guidelines allows teachers to be accountable, but often at the expense of a meaningful curriculum for the students. Many of these teachers long for a relevant, motivating curriculum but they feel constrained.

For optimum student success, the day-to-day curriculum must be both aligned *and* relevant. To create such a curriculum, teachers need to work in two dimensions at the same time. They need to focus both on the Big Picture and the disciplines simultaneously. Figure 1.1 shows a variety of metaphors for this two-dimensional thinking.

Figure 1.1   Two-Dimensional Thinking

BOTH		
Interdisciplinary	←——— AND ———→	Disciplinary
Wide-Angle Lens	←——— AND ———→	Zoom Lens
Connections	←——— AND ———→	Distinctions
Big Picture	←——— AND ———→	Focused Picture
Macro	←——— AND ———→	Micro
Whole	←——— AND ———→	Parts
Jigsaw Puzzle	←——— AND ———→	Jigsaw Pieces

THE KNOW/DO/BE UMBRELLA

To begin to create curriculum that is both relevant and accountable, teachers need a sense of the Big Picture. In a very general sense, what does a K–12 curriculum look like? Are some subject areas more important than others? Do certain knowledge and skills spiral through the curriculum from K to 12? What is most important to learn? Where does the "affect" or student behavior fit into the Big Picture?

An overall view of the purpose of education emerges when one reads all the documents from one jurisdiction using a wide-angle lens. Having done this for several jurisdictions, I am aware that mandated guidelines are quite similar in many ways. Typically, the purpose embedded in the documents is to educate students to be productive citizens in a democratic society. Vermont's framework offers a good example. "Every Vermont student should become a competent, caring, creative, productive, and responsible citizen committed to learning through life" (State of Vermont Department of Education, 2005, p. A5). *Vermont's Framework of Standards and Learning Opportunities* (State of Vermont, 2005) can be accessed through http://www.state.vt.us/educ/new/html/pubs/framework.html.

The overall purpose could be expressed in subject-based documents such as the *North Carolina Standard Course of Study*, which states the following: "The primary purpose of social studies is to help young people develop the ability to make informed decisions for the public good as citizens of a culturally diverse democratic society in an interdependent world" (Public Schools of North Carolina, 2003). This statement is in the *North Carolina Standard Course of Study, Social Studies* (Public Schools of North Carolina, 2003).

When viewing the Big Picture, there is an umbrella over K–12 curriculum. This umbrella represents the core purpose of education and holds within it the most important things for students to know, do, and be during their 13 years in school. Each subject area document is covered by this umbrella and is responsible for developing curriculum within it. Figure 1.2 shows the Know/Do/Be (KDB) Umbrella and its relationship to subject areas.

In most jurisdictions, this umbrella is not explicit. Although many guidelines do recommend interdisciplinary connections, they often do not make these connections explicit. I think there is a very practical reason for this. Most documents are discipline based, and there is no one document that provides an overview. The documents are created for the most part by disciplinary specialists. Because they are usually exemplary educators, they no doubt recognize how interdisciplinary connections can enrich their discipline. However, to create the subject guidelines, they focus on the area of their specialization rather than the Big Picture.

Vermont's Framework of Standards and Learning Opportunities (State of Vermont, 2005) provides a thoughtful overview of the entire curriculum

Figure 1.2   The Know/Do/Be Umbrella

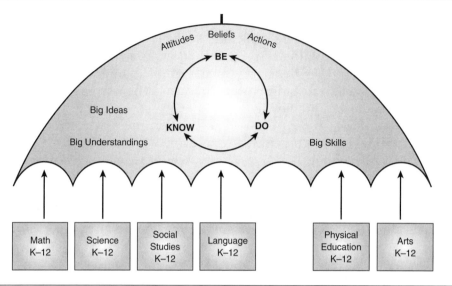

framework. The framework acts as an umbrella for the various disciplinary standards. The framework is divided into "Vital Results" and "Fields of Knowledge." The Vital Results are interdisciplinary and clearly lead toward students becoming productive citizens. The Vital Results include communication, reasoning and problem solving, personal development, and civic and social responsibility. Every subject area can work toward these results. They are the skills and qualities that are considered so important for students to learn that they act as an umbrella for K–12 subject area content. Figure 1.3 offers an overview (an interpretation) of Vermont's framework of Vital Results viewed as a KDB umbrella.

The Ontario Curriculum Grades 11 and 12 Interdisciplinary Studies guideline (Ontario Ministry of Education, 2002), available at http://www.edu .gov.on.ca/eng/document/curricul/secondary/grade1112/inter/inter.htm, offers a different view of the Big Picture. This document allows teachers to bring together two or more existing courses to create a new entity—an interdisciplinary credit. This credit can be issued for the university-bound stream or at the applied level. There is no restriction as to what existing courses can be integrated. The rationale and goals for this credit are disciplinary ones. The standards of such a course transcend the boundaries of disciplines and are unique to interdisciplinary work. An example of this curriculum is in Chapter 7.

Figure 1.4 shows a KDB umbrella for any credit course developed under this plan. A sample curriculum is available online at http://www .curriculum.org/occ/profiles/11/interdisciplinary.shtml. This sample course is called Introduction to Information Studies and integrates the arts, business studies, English, guidance and career education, social studies,

Figure 1.3   An Overview of Vermont's Curriculum Framework Seen as a Know/Do/Be Umbrella

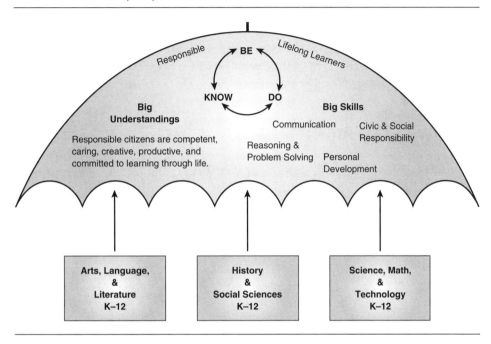

Figure 1.4   A Know/Do/Be Umbrella Based on the *Ontario Curriculum Grades 11 and 12 Interdisciplinary Studies*

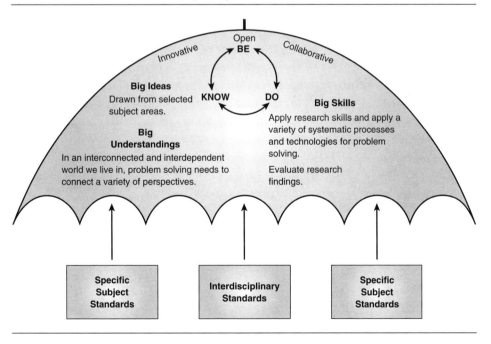

Canadian and world studies, science, and technological studies. It examines the evolution and impact of information, communication, and computing on society from the beginning of writing to the development of the World Wide Web. It was developed by teachers for teachers in partnership with the provincial boards of education and disciplinary associations and was funded by the ministry. It is well worth exploring this sample as a framework for interdisciplinary work.

DESIGNING DOWN

A process called "design down" or "mapping backward" (Wiggins & McTighe, 2005) is a popular and sound way to align disciplinary and interdisciplinary curriculum. I have adapted the design-down approach for interdisciplinary work using the KDB umbrella as the framework. Backward design involves addressing three basic curriculum design questions. These questions are the following:

1. What do I want the students to know, do, and be?

2. What is acceptable evidence to show that they have achieved this?

3. What educational experiences will enable the students to demonstrate the achievement of the KDB?

Often, the first question is not asked with enough emphasis. Educators spend a lot of time working on effective assessment and teaching/learning strategies, but they neglect to ask if what they are teaching and assessing is really significant. Understandably, most teachers accept what is dictated to them in policy documents. These documents rarely help teachers address the question of relative significance. It is up to individual educators to really determine the KDB in their own context—one that allows for designing a curriculum that is relevant to their particular learners. It is also important that these goals be set in a larger context. Thus, we must ask, What is really worth knowing, doing, and being in our world today?

The second question revolves around acceptable evidence to show that the students have learned what they were supposed to learn. For Wiggins and McTighe (2005), this involves developing a core assessment task that demonstrates the core learnings (Enduring Understandings and Big Ideas). Core learnings also involve the skills that are necessary to know to demonstrate the understanding of content. For example, if students are required to do a PowerPoint presentation to communicate their knowledge of content, they may also need to learn the skills needed to create and deliver a PowerPoint presentation. Wiggins and McTighe stress the importance of performance assessments. We cannot know that students know something unless they can do something with what they know (as opposed to a pen-and-paper evaluation such as a standardized test). This second question moves into the area of assessment instruments. We need tools to accurately measure different degrees of student learning. A good rubric, for example, can tell us at what level a student is achieving.

The third question revolves around creating daily learning experiences that will enable the student to achieve the KDB. Learning activities are aligned with standards, and appropriate assessments are integrated into these activities.

DESIGNING DOWN AND INTERDISCIPLINARY WORK

In this book, Chapters 3, 4, and 5 address the three basic questions of backward mapping or designing down. I have presented the process as linear because this is a way to make a complex process understandable. In reality, it is not linear in practice even in disciplinary work. As educators work with one particular step, they need to be able to see the whole, and when they work with the Big Picture, they need to be able to see the parts.

To create the whole, we need more than the three fundamental questions of mapping backward. We need strategies that link the parts together and allow us to move back and forth between the macro and micro elements of curriculum design. To keep the flow of the book, these strategies are introduced throughout the book. These strategies include the following:

- KDB Umbrella
- Scan and Cluster for the KDB
- Exploratory Web
- Big Questions

UNPACKING THE STANDARDS

To understand standards at a deep level, it is necessary to use a zoom lens. The KDB offers a way to unpack or deconstruct a standard. This is not as simple as it sounds. It is very easy to check off a standard as met because it is touched on peripherally during a teaching activity. When one unpacks the standards, it is amazing how complex some of them are. Also, many of them assume that a student already has the skill necessary to achieve the standard. For example, when a student is asked to write a persuasive essay, the teacher needs to be sure that the student has the skills to write such an essay.

To analyze the standards, it is helpful to look at the nouns and verbs. The nouns indicate the *know*. The verbs indicate the *do*. Confusing the issue, some procedural skills such as the scientific method are both a concept and a skill, so the *know* and *do* must be taught. Also, it is informative to look at whether a *be* is explicit or implicit in a standard.

Consider the following preK–12 standards based on *Vermont's Framework of Standards and Learning Opportunities* (State of Vermont, 2005) as presented in Figure 1.5. The verbs have been italicized and the nouns underlined as a way of beginning the task—much like the parsing of a sentence. Unpacking the standards will be explored in greater detail in Chapter 3.

CURRICULUM MAPPING

Curriculum mapping is a popular strategy used by schools and districts to align the curriculum. Essentially, it is a process for recording the content, skills, and assessment actually taught over a distinct learning period or the course of a year. The purpose is to create a seamless curriculum. It is usually done one discipline at a time. Nevertheless, it is an excellent way to begin to think about integrating the curriculum since it identifies gaps and connections.

How do you curriculum map? Mapping is often done at division meetings. It takes time, but it is worthwhile time. Since it is usually done collaboratively, it is a positive step toward building a professional learning community (Truesdale, Thompson, & Lucas, 2004). The conversations that teachers have deepen their understanding of standards and the development of a seamless curriculum. Maps are created horizontally and vertically for each subject area. The process is set out in detail in *Keys to Curriculum Mapping* (Udelhofen, 2005) and *Mapping the Big Picture* (Jacobs, 1997). Many districts in the United States have become involved in the process. Jacobs's *Getting Results With Curriculum Mapping* (2004) offers helpful examples of American educators who are mapping in their contexts.

Christine Shain (www.havergal.on.ca) is an educational consultant who facilitates the curriculum mapping process. Shain offers these suggestions:

- Use available technology to create a map template, or create your own template.
- Identify the *know* and *do*.
- Give enough detail, but not an entire lesson plan.
- Clearly identify what is being taught and assessed.
- Align knowledge and skills with assessment.
- Identify the skills that need to be taught and those that need to be practiced and extended.
- Develop Big Questions that are embedded in the map.

Horizontal Mapping

There is no one way to map the curriculum. Different educators may map in different ways for different purposes. It is important to capture the

Figure 1.5   Unpacking the Standards

Standard	KNOW (nouns)	DO (verbs)	BE
Identify the positive and negative effects of technology.	The positive and negative effects of technology	Identify	Students must make a value judgment on what is negative or positive so they can utilize technology in a way that benefits society.
Students *evaluate* music and music performances.	Evaluation criteria for different categories of music and musical performances	Evaluate	No values are stated, but they are embedded in the evaluation criteria (implicit), so students need to apply these values when they evaluate music and musical performances.
Students *understand* the processes of scientific investigation and *design, conduct, discuss, and evaluate* such investigations.	Scientific investigation processes, procedural steps, how to evaluate their performances, how to communicate these processes	Conduct, communicate, and evaluate scientific investigations.	No values are stated, but if students follow these procedures, they will conduct "objective" investigations that move them closer to the "truth" so objectivity is valued.
Students *understand* the effects of interactions between human and physical systems and *comprehend* the resulting changes in use, distribution, and the significance of resources.	The effects of interactions between human and physical systems Cause-effect cycles	Ambiguous - understanding is vague and does not require a specific skill.	No values are stated although this topic moves into areas such as the human destruction of the environment. Value judgments about results are also necessary.
Students *read and recognize* literature as a record of human experience.	Big Idea of a "record of human experience"	Read literature and identify various examples of "human experience."	Implicitly, literature is valued as a record of human experience.
Students *know* that religious and philosophical ideas have influenced history.	Religious and philosophical ideas, the influence of these throughout history	Nothing	None are identified although this is a value-laden topic so it should engender discernment.

information that is most useful for making curriculum decisions. Usually, there is a horizontal map for each discipline. Most maps include the time frame (full year or unit), content, skills, standards, and assessment. Figure 1.6 offers a sample template showing these categories. For Shain, an excellent map is one that is easily read, is easily shared, and gets to the heart of what is important to teach. Figure 1.7 shows a sample of two units from an excellent curriculum map for a Grade 11 science unit. Seonaid Davis of Havergal College, Toronto, Ontario, created this map using the Ontario curriculum guidelines.

Vertical Mapping

Vertical maps are interesting in that they allow a picture of how the content, skills, and standards are connected and build on each other over the years. In some jurisdictions, curriculum guidelines outline the standards for one strand in one discipline over the succeeding years on one page. Usually these outlines are not for every year, but for every three years or so. It is very helpful to read through this progression in content and skills in the same strand in the same subject area.

Figure 1.8 looks vertically at the *Pennsylvania Code: PA Code 1.8* to point out the similarities across the grades in the broad-based standards for research skills (Commonwealth of Pennsylvania, 2005). These standards can be found in the *Pennsylvania Code* (Commonwealth of Pennsylvania, 2005).

Viewed on one page, there is a startling similarity across the grade levels. Students are learning research from K to 12. It is the same skill with the same components, but obviously the skill needs to be presented differently over the years. Hopefully, the students will recognize research as a basic skill that has the same components regardless of the grade level. Vertical mapping can be done with the same categories as horizontal mapping. Figure 1.9 provides a sample template of a vertical map.

Vertical maps can also be used to focus on how the same skills and concepts are spiraled through the curriculum at a more sophisticated level. Judy Zaenglein of Penn State at Harrisburg has teachers line up against the wall in order of the grade level they teach. Then, together they choose a Big Idea or Big Skill, and each person tells how he or she deals with it at his or her grade level going from the lowest grade to the highest. This way, the teachers get a real sense of a continuum and are ready to map with a Big Picture in mind.

Teachers can look for this progression in skills throughout the documents. Figure 1.10 shows how three Grade 6 teachers began their vertical curriculum mapping process across the disciplines. Christine Shain accomplished something similar when she did curriculum maps with teachers at Pierre LaPorte Middle School, Toronto District School Board, Ontario. They looked for ways that the natural progression of literacy and

(Text continues on page 21)

Figure 1.6   A Generic Curriculum Map for a Discipline

Curriculum Map					

School:

Subject:

Grade Level:

Time Frame	Big Questions	Content	Skills	Standards	Assessment
Sept.					
Oct.					
Nov.					
Dec.					
Jan.					
Feb.					
March					
April					
May					
June					

Figure 1.7 A Sample Curriculum Map for Grade 11 Biology

SBI3U—Grade 11 Biology Map 2004–2005

	Essential Questions	Important Knowledge	Important Skills	Major Assessments
Month September–October **Unit Name** Diversity of Living Things **Throughlines** Structure and Function Evolution Homeostatis	1. Why are there so many different living things? 2. Who are the "Masters of the Universe"?	1. Classification of living things. 2. Identifying features of organisms in the three domains and five kingdoms of life. 3. Introduction to evolutionary theory and natural selection. 4. Natural selection in antibiotic resistance. 5. Characteristics of bacteria and viruses. 6. Bacteria in health and disease. 7. The immune system.	1. Microscope skills 2. Microbiological skills—making agar plates, Kirby-Bauer test for sensitivity. 3. Persuasive essay writing. 4. Planning and conducting an independent experiment and reporting the results. 5. Formal lab writing—introduction, method, results, discussion, proper scientific referencing.	1. Persuasive essay—Who is the master of the universe? 2. Case study—Microbial Pie 3. Public Health report on independent investigations into bacteria. 4. Unit test.
Month November–December **Unit Name** Cell Structure and Function **Throughlines** Structure and Function Evolution Homeostatis	1. How are structure and function related? 2. How do cells work?	1. Very basic chemistry of macromolecules—condensation and hydrolysis reactions. 2. Cell Organelles: nucleus, nucleolus, mitochondria, chloroplast, lysosome, ER, Golgi, vacuoles, robosomes, cell membrane and wall. 3. Cell processes: DNA replication (basic), protein synthesis (basic), cell respiration and photosynthesis (basic), mitosis (review). 4. Structure and function of the cell membrane - how the membrane structure accounts for its transport functions.	1. Identification of macromolecules. 2. Planning and conducting an independent experiment and reporting the results. 3. Formal lab writing - introduction, method, results, discussion, proper scientific referencing. 4. Report writing - summarizing information and writing for a different audience. 5. Interpretation and analysis of data.	1. Cystic fibrosis information pamphlet for parents. 2. Osmosis independent lab investigation. 3. Unit test.

SOURCE: Seonaid Davis.

14

Figure 1.8   A Vertical Curriculum Map for Research Skills

	Research 1.8A	**Research 1.8B**	**Research 1.8C**
Grade 3	Select a topic for research	Locate information using appropriate sources and strategies	Organize and present the main ideas from research
Grade 5	Select and refine a topic for research	Locate information using appropriate sources and strategies	Organize and present the main ideas from research
Grade 8	Select and refine a topic for research	Locate information using appropriate sources and strategies	Organize, summarize, and present the main ideas from research
Grade 11	Select and refine a topic for research	Locate information using appropriate sources and strategies	Organize, summarize, and present the main ideas from research

SOURCE: Commonwealth of Pennsylvania (2005).

Figure 1.9   A Generic Vertical Curriculum Map for One Discipline

School:

Subject:

Year	Standard	Content	Big Skills	Questions	Assessment
2					
3					
4					
5					
6					

Figure 1.10   A Vertical Curriculum Map Created by Grade 6 Teachers

	Grade 4	Grade 5	Grade 7
Language Arts—Writing	*Overall Expectations* Communicate ideas and information for a variety of purposes and to specific audiences.	*Overall Expectations* Communicate ideas and information for a variety of purposes and to specific audiences.	*Overall Expectations* Communicate ideas and information for a variety of purposes and to specific audiences, using forms appropriate for their purpose and topic.
	Organize and develop ideas using paragraphs.	Organize information to convey a central idea, using well-developed paragraphs that focus on a main idea and give some relevant supporting details.	Organize information to develop a central idea, using well-linked and well-developed paragraphs.
	Use correctly the conventions specified for this grade level.	Use correctly the conventions specified for this grade level.	Use correctly the conventions specified for this grade level.
Language Arts—Oral and Visual Communication	*Overall Expectations* Communicate various types of messages, explain some ideas and procedures, and follow the teacher's instructions.	*Overall Expectations* Communicate information, explain a variety of ideas and procedures, and follow the teacher's instructions.	*Overall Expectations* Use instructions and explanations to plan and organize work.
	Communicate a main idea about a topic and describe a short sequence of events.	Communicate a main idea about a topic and describe a short sequence of events.	Listen to and communicate related ideas, and narrate real and fictional events in a sequence.
	Contribute and work constructively in groups.	Contribute and work constructively in groups.	Contribute and work constructively in groups.

	Grade 4	**Grade 5**	**Grade 7**
	Nonverbal Communication Skills	*Nonverbal Communication Skills*	*Nonverbal Communication Skills*
	Use appropriate tone of voice and gestures in social and classroom activities.	Use tone of voice, gestures, and other nonverbal cues to help clarify meaning when describing events, telling stories, reading aloud, making presentations, stating opinions, etc.	Identify some of the ways nonverbal communication techniques can affect audiences, and use these techniques in their own speech to arouse and maintain interest and convince and persuade their listeners.
	Group Skills	*Group Skills*	*Group Skills*
	Listen to others and stay on topic in group discussion. Use appropriate strategies to organize and carry out group projects.	Contribute ideas to help solve problems and listen and respond constructively to the ideas of others when working in a group.	Listen and respond constructively to alternative ideas or viewpoints. Express ideas and opinions confidently but without trying to dominate discussion.
Mathematics— Geometry and Spatial Sense	*Overall Expectations* Identify quadrilaterals and 3-dimensional figures and classify them by their geometric properties, and compare various angles to benchmarks.	*Overall Expectations* Identify and classify 2-dimensional shapes by side and angle properties, and compare and sort 3-dimensional figures.	*Overall Expectations* Construct related lines, and classify triangles, quadrilaterals, and prisms.
	Construct 3-dimensional figures, using 2-dimensional shapes.	Identify and construct nets of prisms and pyramids.	Develop an understanding of similarity, and distinguish similarity and congruence.

(Continued)

Figure 1.10 (Continued)

	Grade 4	Grade 5	Grade 7
	Geometric Properties	*Geometric Properties*	*Geometric Properties*
	Identify and compare different types of quadrilaterals and sort and classify them by their geometric properties.	Distinguish among polygons, regular polygons, and other 2-dimensional shapes.	Construct related lines using angle properties and a variety of tools.
	Identify and describe prisms and pyramids and classify them by their geometric properties using concrete materials.	Distinguish among prisms, right prisms, pyramids, and other 3-dimensional figures.	Sort and classify triangles and quadrilaterals by geometric properties related to symmetry, angles, and sides through investigation using a variety of tools and strategies.
		Identify and classify acute, right, obtuse, and straight angles.	Investigate, using concrete materials, the angles between the faces of a prism, and identify right prisms.
		Measure and construct angles up to 90 degrees, using a protractor.	
		Identify triangles and classify them according to angle and side properties.	
		Construct triangles using a variety of tools, given acute or right angles and side measurements.	
	Geometric Relationships	*Geometric Relationships*	*Geometric Relationships*
	Construct a 3-dimensional figure from a picture or model of the figure, using connecting cubes.	Identify prisms and pyramids from their nets.	Demonstrate an understanding that enlarging or reducing 2-dimensional shapes creates similar shapes.
	Construct skeletons of 3-dimensional figures, using a variety of tools and sketch the skeletons.	Construct nets of prisms and pyramids, using a variety of tools.	

	Grade 4	Grade 5	Grade 7
	Draw and describe nets of rectangular and triangular prisms. Construct prisms and pyramids from given nets. Construct 3-dimensional figures using only congruent shapes.		Distinguish between and compare similar shapes and congruent shapes, using a variety of tools and strategies.
The Arts— Visual Art	*Overall Expectations* Produce 2- and 3-dimensional works of art that communicate ideas (thoughts, feelings, experiences) for specific purposes and to specific audiences. *Knowledge of Elements* Demonstrate awareness that the overlapping of shapes is one way of creating the illusion of depth. *Creative Work* Produce 2- and 3-dimensional works of art that communicate thoughts, feelings, and ideas for specific purposes and to specific audiences.	*Overall Expectations* Produce 2- and 3-dimensional works of art that communicate ideas (thoughts, feelings, experiences) for specific purposes and to specific audiences. *Knowledge of Elements* Identify how the shading of shapes can be used to create the illusion of depth. *Creative Work* Produce 2- and 3-dimensional works of art that communicate thoughts, feelings, and ideas for specific purposes and to specific audiences.	*Overall Expectations* Produce 2- and 3-dimensional works of art that communicate ideas (thoughts, feelings, experiences) for specific purposes and to specific audiences. *Knowledge of Elements* Describe how two-point perspective is used to create the illusion of depth. *Creative Work* Produce 2- and 3-dimensional works of art that communicate a range of thoughts, feelings, and experiences for specific purposes and to specific audiences.

(Continued)

Figure 1.10   (Continued)

	Grade 4	Grade 5	Grade 7
	Identify strengths and areas for improvement in their own work and that of others.	Identify strengths and areas for improvement in their own work and that of others.	Identify strengths and areas for improvement in their own work and that of others. Identify ways in which the visual arts affect various aspects of society and the economy.

SOURCE: Carolyn Bell, Julianne Wiles, and Matthew Lillie.

Figure 1.11   A Curriculum Map Looking for Growth in Reading Strategies Over Time

Grade 6		Grade 7		Grade 8	
Reading strategies	**How assessed?**	**Reading strategies**	**How assessed?**	**Reading strategies**	**How assessed?**
e.g., KWL					
e.g., Anticipation Guide					
What reading strategies have been taught in order to improve comprehension and facilitate depth of understanding in each grade?					
How has their effectiveness been assessed? Remember, assessment includes observation, perceptions, and insights as well as marked work.					
Is there a natural progression that builds comprehension from Grade 6 to Grade 7, and from Grade 7 to Grade 8?					

SOURCE: Christine Shain (http://www.havergal.on.ca).

(Text continued from page 12)

numeracy skills built comprehension over Grades 6 to 8. Figure 1.11 shows the map she used for literacy.

Making Connections Through Mapping

Curriculum mapping often leads to integration projects. Teachers see firsthand the overlap in curriculum standards and unnecessary duplication in their curriculum plans. When Christine Shain was a principal at Gordon Graydon High School, Peel District School Board, Ontario, the Grade 9 math teachers mapped "numeracy skills" and "thinking skills." While discussing how to create an Excel spreadsheet, the teachers realized that they were teaching a lot about place values. Through vertical mapping, they discovered that Grade 10 students learn about variables and that place values are actually variables. Now the Grade 9 teachers can introduce the concept of variables in Grade 9 and tell students that they will be learning more about this concept in Grade 10. This builds a progression in sophistication in learning concepts. As well, teachers discovered that the thinking skills in math were similar to those in literacy. For example, making predictions, seeing between the lines, and solving problems are in both areas. Again, this allowed teachers to make connections across subject areas.

Jacobs (1997, 2004) recommends that cross-disciplinary literacy be mandatory for all students. This requires a consistent focus on (a) building study skills, (b) strategies for interactive text reading, and (c) editing and revising skills. Through curriculum mapping, all classroom teachers should see themselves as teachers of reading, writing, and speaking. Similarly, all teachers are expected to integrate technology across the curriculum.

Mapping naturally leads to a clearer view of both the discipline in focus and the Big Picture. Consider some typical teachers' comments:

- Mapping allows me to identify the essential elements of the curriculum.
- It's easier for me to modify activities from year to year.
- I focus teaching and learning activities and assessments to address what is really important.
- I can build on my colleagues' work.
- Mapping allows me to concentrate on teaching students what they do not know.
- Mapping helps me cluster standards to integrate where appropriate and to articulate essential questions.
- Social studies is a good place to begin curriculum mapping because it encourages integration.
- We can share resources more easily (Miller, 2004).

Curriculum mapping can have powerful results. Lachowicz (2004) describes a two-year curriculum mapping commitment in the Alternative

Education Program, a branch of the Allegheny Intermediate Unit No. 3 in Pittsburg, Pennsylvania. Teachers became more reflective and held higher expectations for themselves and their students. They understood the standards more fully and used them to develop activities that required higher-order thinking. They shifted from writing instructional strategies that began with verbs such as *review, explain,* and *demonstrate* to ones that began with verbs such as *compare and contrast, predict, discover,* and *create*. Assessment techniques were more sophisticated, and the teachers focused on the alignment of assessment, content, and strategies. Finally, they discussed starting points for content integration.

Mapping for Potential Integration

In some jurisdictions, interdisciplinary connections are included on disciplinary curriculum maps. This makes it easier to talk about potential connections. I discussed how to create a horizontal map using Ontario guidelines with Dennis Pikulyk and Roni Sones. We looked for interdisciplinary connections with the existing mandates for Grade 11 Biology using Ontario guidelines. An example of the resulting curriculum map for one unit is shown in Figure 1.12. It is the same unit as shown in Figure 1.7, except that it was created with the explicit idea of moving into interdisciplinary work. The KDB Umbrella was created before the disciplinary map. Thus the standards are deconstructed to identify the *know* (Big Understandings and Ideas) and the *do* (Big Skills). The *be* is implicit in the standards. Potential connections to other subjects are included.

In this chapter, we have explored some basic steps that ensure that the curriculum is aligned. The teachers will be teaching what they are mandated to teach. Presumably, the students will be learning what they are mandated to learn. What may be missing in these recipes for accountability is the relevance factor. Many people, myself included, believe that if the curriculum is not relevant to students, they will not learn it in a way that sticks. Advocates of interdisciplinary approaches to curriculum believe that integration is the route to relevance. But what does interdisciplinary curriculum look like in an age of accountability? The next chapter explores this question.

DISCUSSION QUESTIONS

1. Discuss the different types of accountability. How do these play out in your local context?

2. Discuss Figure 1.1 and how two-dimensional thinking plays out in curriculum planning in your context or experience.

3. For many teachers, the backward design process is difficult to follow. They prefer to identify good teaching strategies first and

Figure 1.12   A Sample of a Curriculum Map That Focuses on Connections in One Unit of Grade 11 Biology

	Big Questions Topic	Interdisciplinary Connections	KNOW (from standards)	DO (from standards)	BE
Sept/Oct Unit Name *Diversity of Living Things*	*Big Questions:* How are structure and function related? How is evolution supported? *Topic Questions:* Why are there so many different living things? Who are the "Masters of the Universe"?	*Art* Microscope skills, line drawing, representational art *Geography* Plant/animal species unique to certain parts of the world (evolution, structure) Continental Drift *Math* Equations to support evolution Hardy-Weinburg law *Technology* Simulation of natural selection *History/philosophy* Eugenics Genetic disease Pedigrees (hemophilia) Russian Revolution *English* Report writing Persuasive writing	*Big Understandings:* The structure of an organism allows it to fulfill its function. Evolution is supported by substantive evidence. *Big Ideas: Structure and function Evolution* 1. classification 2. features of 3 domains & 5 kingdoms 3. intro to evolution & natural selection 4. characteristics of bacteria & viruses 5. bacteria in health and disease 6. immune system	*Big Skills: Scientific method* Microscope skills Microbiological skills Independently plan and conduct and report experiment on bacteria Formal lab writing *Persuasive essay*	*Think critically* *Objective* when doing experiments and lab writing *Persuasive* when writing persuasive essay *Work co-operatively*

SOURCE: Christine Shain (http://www.havergal.on.ca).

then go on to design the curriculum. What is the difference when teachers do use backward design?

4. Curriculum mapping is a good preparation for integrating the curriculum. What are the advantages? Can you see how it might fit in your context?

5. What do Figure 1.8 and Figure 1.10, tell us about the nature of standards?

SUGGESTED ACTIVITIES

1. Look up your state (or provincial) standards on the Internet. Is there a framework that acts as a KDB Umbrella? In other words, has the state identified the most important knowledge and skills that they expect a student to demonstrate from K to 12? Have they done this for a selected group of grades (e.g., 9–12)? Have they done this for individual subjects such as science and geography?

2. Look up another state (or province) and compare it to yours. In what ways is the framework the same? different?

3. Unpacking the standards is an important skill to ensure that you are actually teaching what the standard requires. Create a chart such as Figure 1.5. Using relevant standards, choose one or two standards from each subject. Deconstruct the *know*, *do*, and *be*.

2

What Is Interdisciplinary Curriculum?

W hat is *integrated* or *interdisciplinary curriculum?* A definition is particularly elusive. The York University example on the first page of the Preface offers the essence of interdisciplinary approaches—looking at things from more than one perspective. In this book, the terms *integrated* and *interdisciplinary* will be used interchangeably to generically describe a curriculum that connects the various disciplines in some way. In this chapter, we will explore different definitions of interdisciplinary curriculum and what they mean in practice.

Educators can conceive of curriculum integration in a wide variety of ways, and its implementation can be unique in every setting. Virtually any combination of subjects can be integrated given the will of the teachers involved. Perhaps one teacher teaches several subjects through a universal concept or theme. Or perhaps a team of teachers combines areas of expertise. This is one of the pitfalls of interdisciplinary approaches—they cannot be standardized or rarely even replicated by another set of teachers who wish to do the same thing. On the other hand, one of the greatest appeals of integration is this lack of a standardized definition. Teachers can be creative. They can set the curriculum in a relevant context. They can craft it around the needs of their students. They can even ask for students' input into what students want to learn. The ways to make connections across subject areas are limitless. This is both frightening and exhilarating for teachers.

This chapter will explore how integrated curriculum was conceived in the late 1980s and early 1990s and where we have gone from there. This exploration will offer a good starting point for understanding what integrated curriculum can be. It also offers a way to see how one could begin to create an integrated curriculum in an age of standards, accountability, and standardized testing.

The last part of the chapter will show how current interdisciplinary approaches are different from, yet similar to, their predecessors of the past.

LOOKING BACK AT THE LATE 1980s AND EARLY 1990s

Interdisciplinary approaches to curriculum flourished in the late 1980s and early 1990s. At that time, critics of education said that schools were not preparing students well enough to be productive citizens of the twenty-first century. The fault lay, in part, in the lack of relevant curriculum. Young people were not learning because they could not find personal meaning in their studies.

Interdisciplinary approaches seemed to address not only the relevance problem but many other contextual factors as well. Teachers could set the curriculum in a real-life context that presumably would capture students' attention. This allowed for teacher creativity and honored them as intelligent agents of education. An interdisciplinary approach would eliminate duplication found across subject areas. Research about how students learned best seemed to favor integrated curriculum. According to brain research, the brain thrives on variety and processes most effectively when it makes connections (Jensen, 2005). Also, interdisciplinary approaches left open the possibilities of applying popular learning theories such as multiple intelligences and learning styles.

It was a time when the potential of the Internet was just being acknowledged. The exponential explosion of knowledge offered yet another reason to adopt an approach that did not attempt to teach "everything." Supporters claimed that interdisciplinary approaches allowed for studying a concept in depth as opposed to breadth. It was also becoming increasingly clear that knowledge did not belong in carefully defined boxes called "disciplines." Some of the boxes were already overflowing and were subdivided into subdisciplines, such as in biotechnology, medical physics, and astrophysics in the sciences. In fact, knowledge in the disciplines seemed to overlap into a messy, interconnected, and interdependent blur.

Some jurisdictions leapt into interdisciplinary approaches. In Ontario, for example, the new curriculum documents mandated integrated curriculum from K to 9. Few people actually knew how to develop an integrated curriculum. They were confounded by the lack of a clear definition or clear direction. Also, practitioners encountered all the predictable problems that go with any major change. In short, these were turbulent times. During this period, I was very involved helping people understand, design, and implement such curriculum.

It was clear to everyone that there were a variety of ways to approach integration. One of the major theoretical questions at the time was whether the approaches were hierarchal. Many theorists agreed that there was definitely a range of approaches that appeared to be hierarchal in that they became more and more integrated (Drake, 1993; Erickson, 2001; Jacobs, 1989). A common way to see this hierarchal range is illustrated in Figure 2.1.

Robin Fogarty (1991) offered 10 different interpretations of curriculum integration, as shown in Figure 2.2. Applying her chart, teachers could make sense of their own practices in light of the 10 possibilities. For example, most elementary teachers were already teaching similar skills such as literacy across the curriculum. Teachers in the higher grades could see how different skill sets appeared in different subject areas. This opened the door to new understandings of the potential for integration.

Fogarty's 10 positions did not exactly fit my own experience as the leader of a provincial curriculum team developing integrated curriculum. For me, her last two examples were not integration because students experienced connections during independent studies. Her other eight positions did not seem to match my team's experience of trying to develop a full-blown curriculum. The 10 positions described parts within the whole.

My team's definition of integration shifted as we worked on creating a curriculum document (Drake, 1991). We experienced three major shifts that felt profound. These shifts included changes in philosophy, in our perceptions of how knowledge and skills were interconnected, and in our ideas about assessment. Most important, our task of creating integrated curriculum was startlingly different depending on which shift we were in. We discovered that we were not the first people to experience these three

Figure 2.1   Different Approaches to Integration as a Hierarchy

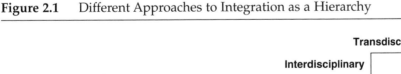

Figure 2.2   Robin Fogarty's 10 Approaches to Integration

1

Fragmented
Periscope—one direction; one sighting; narrow focus on single discipline

Description
The traditional model of separate and distinct disciplines, which fragments the subject areas.

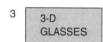

Example
Teacher applied this view in Math, Science, Social Studies, Language Arts, OR Sciences, Humanities, Fine and Practical Arts.

2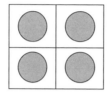

Connected
Opera Glass—details of one discipline; focus on subtleties and interconnections

Description
Within each subject area, course content is connected topic to topic, concept to concept, one year's work to the next, and relates idea(s) explicitly.

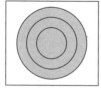

Example
Teacher relates the concept of fractions to decimals, which in turn relates to money, grades, etc.

3

Nested
3-D glasses—multiple dimensions to one scene, topic, or unit

Description
Within each subject area, the teacher targets multiple skills, a social skill, a thinking skill, and a content-specific skill.

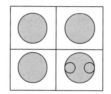

Example
Teacher designs the unit on photosynthesis to simultaneously target consensus seeking (social skills), sequencing (thinking), and plant life cycle (science content).

4

Sequenced
Eyeglasses—varied internal content framed by broad, related concepts

Description
Topics or units of study are rearranged and sequenced to coincide with one another. Similar ideas are taught in concert while remaining separate subjects.

Example
English teacher presents an historical novel depicting a particular period while the History teacher teaches that same historical period.

5 **BINOCULARS**

Shared
Binoculars—two disciplines that share overlapping concepts and skills

Description
Shared planning and teaching take place in two disciplines in which overlapping concepts or ideas emerge as organizing elements.

Example
Science and Math teachers use data collection, charting, and graphing as shared concepts that can be team-taught.

6 **TELESCOPE**

Webbed
Telescope—broad view of entire constellation as one theme, webbed to the various elements

Description
A fertile theme is webbed to curriculum contents and disciplines; subjects use the theme to sift out appropriate concepts, topics, and ideas.

Example
Teacher presents a simple topical theme, such as the circus, and webs it to the subject areas. A conceptual theme, such as conflict, can be webbed for more depth in the theme approach.

7 **MAGNIFYING GLASS**

Threaded
Magnifying Glass—big ideas that magnify all content through a metacurricular approach

Description
The metacurricular approach threads thinking skills, social skills, multiple intelligences, technology, and study skills through the various disciplines.

Example
Teaching staff targets prediction in Reading, Math, and Science lab experiments while Social Studies teacher targets forecasting current events, and thus threads the skill (prediction) across disciplines.

8 **KALEIDOSCOPE**

Integrated
Kaleidoscope—new patterns and designs that use the basic elements of each discipline

Description
This interdisciplinary approach matches subjects for overlaps in topics and concepts with some team teaching in an authentic integrated model.

Example
In Math, Science, Social Studies, Fine Arts, Language Arts, and Practical Arts teachers look for patterning models and approach content through these patterns.

(Continued)

Figure 2.2 (Continued)

9

Immersed
Microscope—
intensely personal
view that allows
microscopic
explanation as all
content is filtered

Description
The disciplines become part of the learner's
lens of expertise; the learner filters all content
through this lens and becomes immersed in
his or her own experience.

Example
Student or doctoral candidate has
an area of expert interest and sees
all learning through that lens.

10

Networked
Prism—a view that
creates multiple
dimensions and
directions of
focus

Description
Learner filters all learning through the expert's
eye and makes internal connections that lead to
external networks of experts in related fields.

Example
Architect, while adopting the
CAD/CAM technology for design,
networks with technical programmers
and expands her knowledge base,
just as she had traditionally done
with interior designers.

SOURCE: Adapted with permission of the publisher in Fogarty (1991), extrapolated from Jacobs (1989, pp. 1–3).

different positions, and there was a common language for them—multidisciplinary, interdisciplinary, and transdisciplinary.

Were any of these positions superior to the others? At that time, I was convinced that one position was not superior to another, but that each orientation offered advantages in different contexts and for different purposes (Drake, 1993). In today's context, when all approaches need to be standards based, this controversy is not really relevant. Each approach is as valid as another as long as it honors accountability mandates.

No matter the approach, connections are made around a topic, theme, concept, problem, or issue. There is some controversy about what makes a better organizer. Educators claim that organizing curricula around a topic like "pioneers" or "bears" leads to superficial curricula because teachers could do a trivial activity like counting the number of bears in a picture book and claim to have added "math" to their unit. To ensure depth, a curriculum needs to be organized around richer concepts. In Chapter 3, the development of rich concepts is discussed in detail.

DEGREES OF INTEGRATION

As was shown in Figure 2.1 and Figure 2.2, there are degrees of integration. For the purposes of definition, we will look at four degrees of integration. Each one reflects a higher degree of integration in the number of connections that are made and the time dedicated to it.

Fusion

One of the first steps on the integration ladder is fusion. Here, something is fused to the already existing curriculum. For example, groups who represent teachers of history have built a case for infusing history into reading programs and instruction at large (King & Zucker, 2005; Manzo, 1996). Why? An unintended consequence of the No Child Left Behind Act has been that the emphasis on improving reading and math test scores has pushed history into a marginalized position. Teachers looking for more time to spend on language and math activities tend to pinch it from social studies, art, and physical education. Social studies teachers say that as a result, students are not learning how to be engaged citizens of their community. The infusion of history would mean that it is taught in every class.

At Evanston Township High School, in Evanston, Illinois, global studies are infused into the school curriculum. Because the curricula across subject areas are internationally focused, students gain a deep understanding of world issues from a variety of subject-specific viewpoints. All 150 students learn Japanese. Even the extracurricular program takes on a global perspective with events such as Islamic Awareness and hosting a Japanese tea. On a typical day in the Middle Eastern studies class, students prepared for the Iraqi elections. Israeli hip hop music played in the background as Islamists and Royalists readied their promotional material. Members of the Kurdish Democratic Party put on their Kurdish hats. The speeches began with the Iraqi national Congress members pleading for a democratic Iraq (Paulson, 2005).

At Benjamin Franklin Middle School in Ridgewood, New Jersey, a variety of teaching approaches are implemented, but the social and emotional components of a child's life are considered most important. In every conceivable way, the organization of the school is designed to show students that the adults care about them. The school has adopted a social and emotional learning (SEL) program developed by Maurice Elias at Rutgers University to guide this fusion (Curtis, 2003). The principal leads meetings with parents, students, and teachers to discuss and commit to SEL. Each child is touched by several SEL experiences daily. The students begin each day with a period devoted to building community. They belong to teams and have as much access to their team teachers as possible. Parents are encouraged to be highly involved as partners, and there is even a Parent Center on campus. In sports, there is a "no-cut" policy: All children can play. Although the school competes against other schools, there is no "elite" team.

A centerpiece of the school is the Grade 8 production of a community service television program called *Benjamin Franklin Broadcast News*. The daily show features student news and a public service spot. This spot stems from student research, and the content often reflects character development themes. The production involves teamwork, goal setting, planning, listening, and cooperation. This program alone demonstrates integration through SEL on multiple levels. A detailed description of this program is available on the "Teaching in the Digital Age: Emotional Intelligence" videocassette available from the George Lucas Foundation and is profiled in an article by Diane Curtis (2003) that was published in the *Eutopia* newsletter (www.glef.org).

Evanston Township High School and Benjamin Franklin Middle School are examples of integration through fusion.

Multidisciplinary

In the multidisciplinary approach, disciplines remain very distinct, but deliberate connections are made between or among them. See Figure 2.3 for a graphic of an organizing center. At the elementary level, students may visit different learning centers to study a theme. For example, students may

Figure 2.3   Multidisciplinary Organizing Center

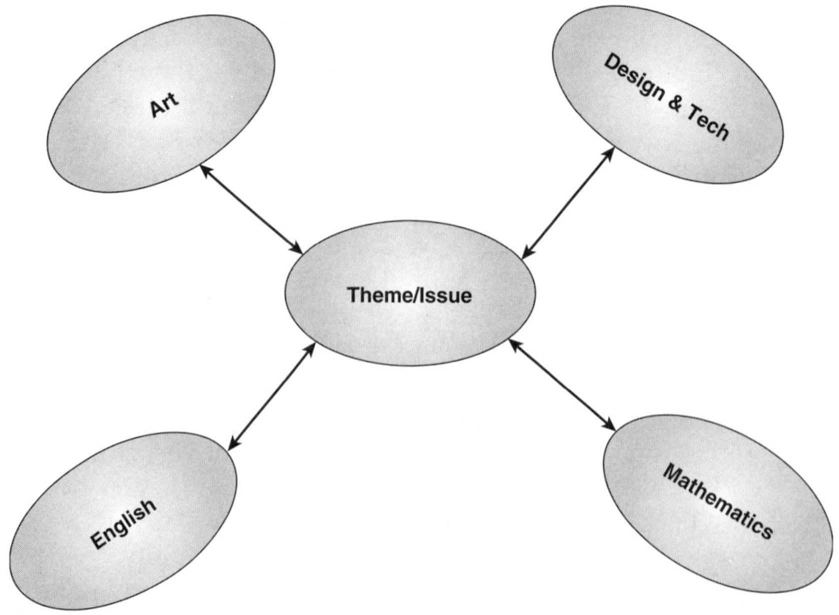

study "communities" and engage in disciplinary activities, rotating through a social studies center, a language arts center, an arts center, a math center, and a science center. In high school, the students may study a similar theme in their different classrooms. A typical example is students studying the American Civil War in history and simultaneously reading *The Red Badge of Courage* in English. The Civil War theme may arise in drama class and visual arts or other subject areas. Sometimes this is called *parallel curriculum*. The same subject matter is taught at the same time.

From the multidisciplinary perspective, teachers do not need to make very many changes. Content and assessment remain firmly within an intact subject. Generally, students are expected to make the connections among subject areas, rather than the teachers having taught them explicitly. Figure 2.4 shows the planning template for a parallel curriculum. The KDB umbrella represents the K–12 grade for the particular jurisdiction.

Yet within this perspective, there are also degrees of integration. Some multidisciplinary approaches make stronger connections, and when the subject boundaries begin to blur, the curriculum shifts into interdisciplinary territory. The work of Kathleen Harris offers a good example. Harris runs Harris Consulting, Inc., with the Small Schools Workshop (Ksmachar@aol.com). She has worked with schools all over the United States. Harris has teams of teachers who work together to decide on a common concept and subconcept that they will teach. Next, they plan an integrated assessment to culminate the unit. Finally, these teachers develop and teach in their disciplines the knowledge and skills that lead to the culminating activity. Harris's framework is standards based and all decisions are guided by the standards. See Figure 2.5 for a planning template for this version of multidisciplinary curriculum.

Riverview High School in Sarasota, Florida, offers various "academies" that run thematic programs. In the Championship Academy, Grade 10 students experienced a multidisciplinary unit called "prediction" based on Harris's work. The teachers chose "prediction" as the main concept that they all would teach. The subconcept was "recruitability"; the common skill was "critical thinking." The teachers wanted students to demonstrate self-discipline. Next, the teachers created an integrated authentic activity: You are a scout or coach for your favorite college, and you are to predict or determine the recruitability of a football player (or a swimmer) based on character traits, behavior, grades, physical ability, and athletic (sport-specific) ability.

In each classroom, students completed a representative task that led to the integrated authentic activity. They did the following:

- Read Act 1 in Julius Caesar and predicted further actions through character analysis (language arts).
- Predicted what would happen in muscle cells when exercise became aerobic (biology).
- Graphically predicted the outcome values of given variables (math).

Figure 2.4   A Planning Template for Parallel Disciplines

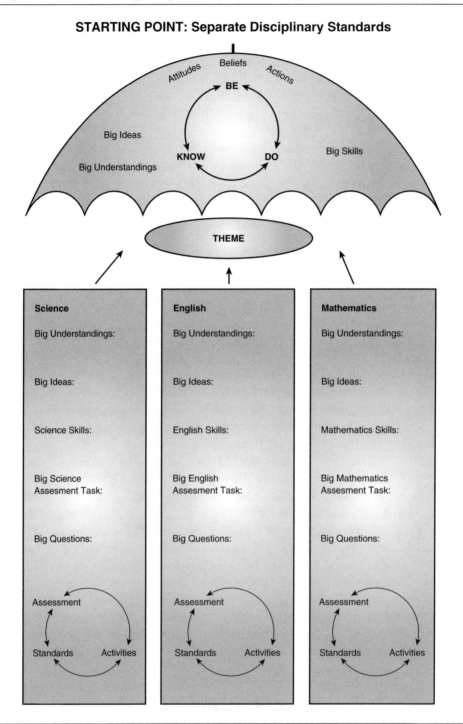

Figure 2.5   A Planning Template for Multidisciplinary Curriculum With an
Integrated Assessment Task

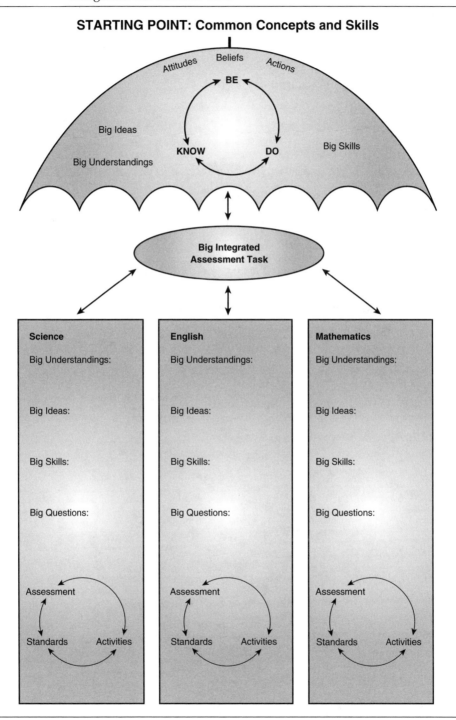

- Researched sports and wellness careers and predicted areas of future interest to them (journalism).
- Predicted in Spanish the impact of being able to communicate in another language on a future career in sports (Spanish).

These examples from Kathleen Harris and Riverview High School demonstrate the multidisciplinary approach.

Interdisciplinary

The interdisciplinary curriculum makes more explicit connections across the subject areas. Again, the curriculum revolves around a common theme, issue, or problem, but interdisciplinary concepts or skills are emphasized across the subject areas rather than within them. For example, the unit may be organized around a universal concept, such as conflict or change, or may emphasize generic research skills. See Figure 2.6 to see an organizing center for interdisciplinary curriculum.

An example of the interdisciplinary approach is Grade 10 students at Lower Canada College in Quebec who used Web technology to study Shakespeare (Kee, 2005). Students selected one soliloquy or passage from *Macbeth*. Their task was to write a Web essay that demonstrated their basic understanding of important concepts. Through hypertext links, they

Figure 2.6   Interdisciplinary Organizing Center

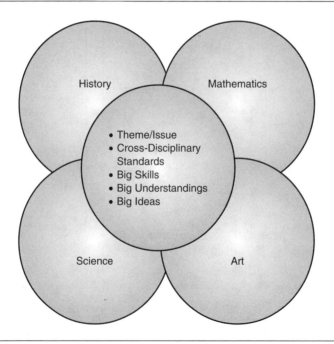

History

Mathematics

- Theme/Issue
- Cross-Disciplinary Standards
- Big Skills
- Big Understandings
- Big Ideas

Science

Art

created deeper levels of connection and demonstrated analysis, synthesis, and evaluation skills. Finally, they made a video for the Web showing their critical thinking skills. Working in groups of four, students also needed to work collaboratively. This example shows the emphasis on skills as the common denominator across the curriculum.

John Hersey High School in Chicago (suburban, middle class, mostly white) and Chicago International Charter School Northtown Academy Campus (low-income, minority, urban students) implemented an interdisciplinary curriculum that also integrates traditional expectations (Ferrero, 2006). Teachers carefully map the skills and content necessary to succeed at the ACT college readiness standards and standardized diagnostic assessments through a vertical mapping of the curriculum. Students are grouped by ability to learn the core content and master these skills. These skills are considered the foundation for higher-order thinking and are necessary for all students when they participate during the year in integrated units that include all students in any given grade level. Students are expected to participate fully in the integrated units and are involved in hands-on projects.

The success of this interdisciplinary/traditional approach is dramatic. Hersey's average ACT test scores rose from the 60th percentile in 2000 to the 75th in 2005. Student growth on benchmarked performances rose approximately 71%. For every 100 students who entered Grade 9 as a remedial student, more than 50% enrolled in college prep or honor courses by the 11th grade. Most gains are in reading and writing where the model is most fully developed. Northtown's students have been similarly successful. With the help of the Bill and Melinda Gates Foundation, the Chicago Charter School Foundation with Civitas schools plans to expand the model to other schools.

Figure 2.7 offers a planning template for interdisciplinary curriculum where the common knowledge and skills are the starting point. There is an integrated Big Assessment task. The disciplines are not as discrete as they are in the multidisciplinary approach.

Transdisciplinary

This approach begins with a real-life context. It does not begin with the disciplines or with common concepts or skills. What is usually considered most important is the perceived relevance for the students. Figure 2.8 shows an organizing center for transdisciplinary curriculum.

The planning template for transdisciplinary curriculum (Figure 2.9) is similar to the one offered in Figure 2.7. The difference is the starting point because the emphasis is on a real-world context and on student interests.

The International School of the Americas is a charter school of about 460 students in San Antonio, Texas. This school is intent on providing students with the academic knowledge and skills to work in a global context and "to change the world" (Albright & Breidenstein, 2004). The school offers a rich, integrated curriculum. Students choose an international

Figure 2.7   A Planning Template for Interdisciplinary Curriculum

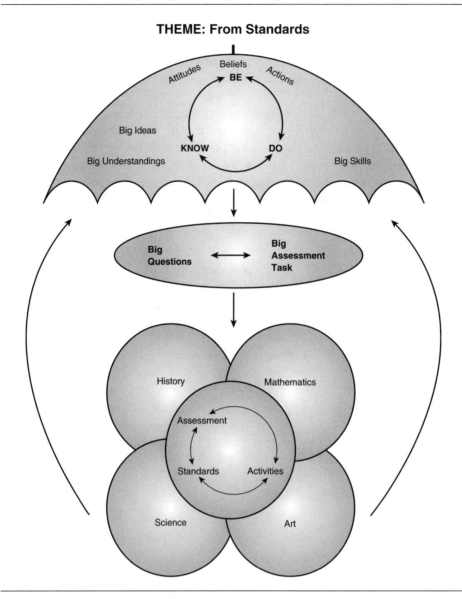

challenge and conduct research, prepare an informative Web page, design and implement a service-learning project, and present their findings to a panel of community judges. Topics they have covered range from homelessness to teen alcohol abuse. Some of the teaching is traditional. However, all students go on travel expeditions. Each grade visits a specific destination to learn firsthand about an international issue. As freshmen, for example, they travel to Heifer International Airport in Arkansas where they live for four days experiencing the challenge of economic need and learn about sustainable economic development.

Figure 2.8   Transdisciplinary Organizing Center

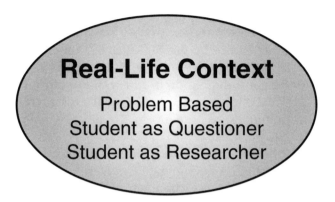

Figure 2.9   A Planning Template for a Transdisciplinary Curriculum

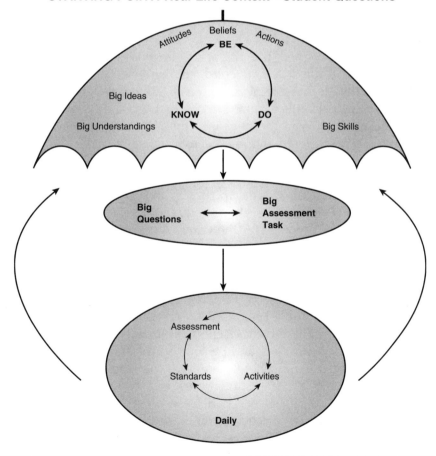

Sylvia Moore runs an interesting multiage enrichment project at North Queens Elementary School in Nova Scotia for Grades 4, 5, and 6. The school is in a small, rural community located just outside the boundaries of a national park and within the southwest Nova Biosphere Reserve. The area has a long history of use by the Mi'kmaq Nation, and there is a First Nations community within the school boundaries. Early settlers to the area harvested the forests, and the region is still well known for logging, lumber mills, and Christmas tree farms. There is also a research institute in the community, and many researchers are in the area on a short-term basis doing research at the park.

Recently, the students produced a video documentary about forests based on their research. The documentary investigated three worldviews of forests in the biosphere reserve: the scientific worldview, the indigenous perspective, and local ecological knowledge. The topics on the documentary ranged from tree growth and tree types to harvesting methods and monitoring efforts. Some people spoke about the spirituality of forests and touched on their personal views as well as on larger environmental issues. The project involved science, social studies, language arts, drama, and technology. Curriculum outcomes were a compilation of cross-curricular objectives from the respective curriculum guides at each grade level. Each student created a portfolio that included artifacts from this program. Assessment focused on this portfolio.

The students designed the research questions, arranged interview times both on and off site, and conducted interviews and videotaped them. In class, they learned to develop questions and practiced interviews and the technological skills required to conduct the taping. After the interviews, the class discussed the new information they learned from each interviewee. They explored the perspective of the speaker and how this information on forests augmented or contradicted what they had learned to this point.

Through hikes in the woods and visits to research and monitoring sites, students experienced forests directly. Some students traveled in a helicopter to get aerial footage for the video. A number rode in a harvester with a forestry crew who were cutting on a local woodlot. All students worked with a Mi'kmaq dance and theatre director who supported the students through the writing of skits that highlighted the issues they were learning about in their research. In addition, students made drums and learned several songs with a Mi'kmaq elder.

The video was premiered at the school on June 21, National Aboriginal Day. Students sang, drummed, and performed the skits to begin the day's events. In addition to the school premiere, the documentary has been shown to visitors at the local national park and at a public forum at the research institute. The project was a rich learning experience for all concerned including students, teacher, parents, and community participants.

A fascinating aspect of this project was that the students created material that is now a teacher resource for use in other classrooms. This goes far beyond the concept of authentic assessment, in which a real-world audience assesses the students. These students now teach teachers and provide them with material to use when teaching other students. This is truly collaborative learning with student-student and student-teacher learning occurring. The collaboration extended to community members. Even highly regarded scientists were fellow learners. The final product of the learning, the video documentary, reflected this shared learning and placed students in a leadership role as the producers of learning materials.

An influential educator in the transdisciplinary area is James Beane (1993, 1997). He advocates that the curriculum be developed from the interests of the students themselves. For him, these questions can be categorized as personal growth or social issues. Brown (2006) also recommends that students create their own curriculum based on their own questions. He suggests that in this way, students will learn and apply higher-order thinking skills that prepare them for the world of work. His experience demonstrates that students can and do ask substantive questions that revolve around:

- Environmental issues
- Making and managing money
- Future technology
- How to make the world a peaceful place
- Prejudice
- Power—Who has it and how is it managed?
- Crime and violence
- What does the future hold for me?

The Alpha program is an exemplary example of what can happen when Beane's (1993, 1997) and Brown's (2006) philosophies are applied. The Alpha program is a school within a school at Shelburne Community School in Shelburne, Vermont. Operating since 1972, this alternative, multiage middle school has withstood the test of time. Curricula are developed from student questions, thus ensuring relevance. Students brainstorm their own questions and create themes for study. At the same time, they are aware of the standards. Coplanning with their teachers and using their selected themes, the students develop three standards-based units for the year. Typical themes have been "We the People" (government), careers, and conflict resolution. Students plan the activities and the assessments. Evaluation is an important part of the program. Two examples of the programs done before 1993 that are well described are "Adopt a Business" and "The Big Alpha Circus" (Stevenson & Carr, 1993). These are rich examples of integrated curriculum. More recent detailed descriptions of the process are also available (Drake & Burns, 2004; Smith & Myers, 2001).

A SUMMARY OF THE DIFFERENT APPROACHES TO INTEGRATION

The process of creating interdisciplinary work has changed since the 1980s and 1990s because teachers must teach to the standards. Although it may seem to be the same process on the surface, decidedly, it is not. One can still identify fusion and multidisciplinary, interdisciplinary, and transdisciplinary approaches.

In an age of accountability, however, the different approaches of integrated curriculum blur as teachers apply the standards-based principles to integration. There are certain rules that seem to go hand in hand with accountability mandates. These rules begin with the requirement that the teacher must cover the standards and prepare students for required standardized tests. Across North America, the process of designing down or

Figure 2.10   Comparing and Contrasting the Different Interdisciplinary Approaches

How Do Various Approaches Differ?		
Approach	**Starting Point Intentions**	**Primary Assessment Concern**
Fusion	A focus that is embedded into all school life. Some examples are environmental stewardship, international education, and social-emotional learning.	Assessment remains subject specific.
Multidisciplinary	The concepts and skills of the disciplines	Disciplinary concepts and skills
Interdisciplinary	Common concepts and skills across the disciplines	Common concepts and skills across the disciplines
Transdisciplinary	Real-world context and student questions life skills	Authentic assessment in a real life context
What Is the Same Among All Approaches?		
Fusion	✓ Mapping backwards design—using standards ✓ Exemplary teaching/learning strategies ✓ Set in a student-relevant real-world context as much as possible ✓ Performance demonstrations as well as standardized assessment	
Multidisciplinary		
Interdisciplinary		
Transdisciplinary		

mapping backwards is very popular for designing any curriculum, whether it be within a discipline or interdisciplinary. At the same time, curriculum designers can use the best teaching and learning strategies to enable the students to meet the standards.

Figure 2.10 shows how the different approaches blur when a teacher plans using the standards-based rules.

In the chapter, we have looked at different approaches to integrated curriculum. The first part dealt with how these positions looked in the late 1980s and early 1990s. Then we looked at how these positions changed with the advent of standards and standardized testing. In the next chapter, we will begin to explore how to create interdisciplinary curriculum.

DISCUSSION QUESTIONS

1. How does a brief history of curriculum integration help your understanding?

2. Examine Fogarty's 10 approaches to integration. Describe any that you have experienced either as a student or as an educator.

3. What is the main difference among multidisciplinary, inter-disciplinary, and transdisciplinary approaches?

4. Compare the templates in Figures 2.4 and 2.6. How much difference do you think the variation in planning would make to the end product? Can you think of other examples of ways that teachers might apply Figure 2.6 in different contexts?

5. Discuss Figure 2.10 and its implications for curriculum design.

SUGGESTED ACTIVITIES

1. Read the examples for multidisciplinary, interdisciplinary, and transdisciplinary curricula. Using your local standards, select a content area and theme for an integrated unit based on two or more subjects. How would this unit look if you taught it from the multidisciplinary, interdisciplinary, and transdisciplinary perspectives?

2. Using Figure 2.10, describe how these three different approaches to the same unit would be similar.

3

What Do We Want Students to Know, Do, and Be?

Wʜe are moving from an industrial society into a knowledge society (Hargreaves, 2003). The knowledge base is exponentially increasing, and there is simply too much for any one person to know today. As educators, how do we choose what students need to know in the knowledge society? How can we predict what people will need to be able to do in a rapidly changing world? The Internet alone has opened up a new world of necessary technological skills students must acquire to navigate the complex knowledge society.

At this time, most curriculum documents deal with what a student should know and do to be a productive citizen in a democratic society. Yet there is little mention of how we want our students to become productive citizens in a democratic society. What are the desired attitudes, beliefs, and behaviors? Do our students, for example, demonstrate the habits of mind? Some educators feel ambivalent about including the *be* because this area is difficult to measure. For others, the question revolves around whose values would or should be imposed on our students.

It is important to reflect on how we want people to be as humans. How do we want our students to be in our classrooms and in the world? We are living in a global age. We need to be able to get along with our neighbors rather than live under a constant threat, whether of terrorism, war, or local misunderstandings. The word *democracy* is often used to describe the goals of education. *Democratic* is a value-laden word that describes how we want a person to be in our society.

How do we think about the Know, Do, Be (KDB) from an interdisciplinary perspective? This will be explored using a wide-angle lens.

USING THE WIDE-ANGLE LENS TO FIND THE KDB: SEEING THE BIG PICTURE

What Is Worth Knowing?

Our modern world challenges us to reexamine the essential educational question: "What is worth knowing?" Schools have been charged not only with responsibility for their traditional subject areas but also with such cross-disciplinary topics as multiculturalism, antiviolence, gender equity issues, racism, AIDS education, and conflict resolution. The list seems endless. Some people argue that we should teach only the classics such as Shakespeare; others insist that we include popular culture. In a culture in which North American students watch many hours of television and are profoundly influenced by media, media literacy seems crucial. Living in a global world, students need to have a global perspective. Having an educated approach to contemporary issues seems essential for the productive citizen of the twenty-first century.

To really understand what is worth knowing, one needs to be familiar with the structure of knowledge (Figure 3.1). Based on Hilda Taba's work, Erickson (2001) suggests that knowledge moves up from facts at the base of the hierarchy to topics, disciplinary concepts (big disciplinary ideas), universal concepts (Big Ideas), and essential understandings (Big Understandings). At the top of the pyramid is theory.

The *know* is not independent from the *do*. The *do* skills are interdisciplinary processes that learners require to move up the hierarchy of knowledge. Reading, writing, computing, drawing, dramatizing, thinking, and listening are developmental processes that become more complex and sophisticated throughout an educational career and indeed throughout life. According to Erickson (2001), as we move higher on the structure of knowledge, we also move up from a lower to a higher level of skills from memorizing to analyzing, synthesizing, creating, and hypothesizing. Thus, only when a student works in the conceptual realm can he or she be a critical thinker, one of the most desired but least defined goals of education.

Big Ideas

In interdisciplinary work, universal concepts, or Big Ideas and Big Understandings, are the most important thing to know. A universal concept

Figure 3.1   The Structure of Knowledge and the Interaction of the *Know* and the *Do*

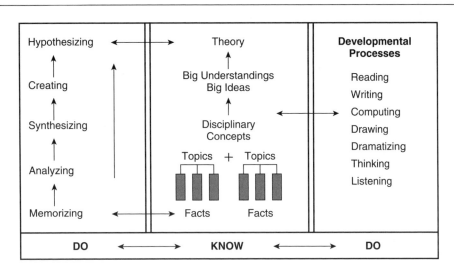

is broad and abstract. It transcends the disciplines and cultures. It is represented by one or two words, and it is timeless and universal in application. Not all concepts are universal. Some are discipline-bound concepts such as pulleys and gears. Although students will definitely be learning disciplinary concepts, it is the broader concepts that we are interested in to act as a KDB umbrella across the disciplines.

Big Idea is a descriptive term that teachers and students like and understand easily. Generally, the term *Big Idea* is used to describe concepts at both levels—disciplinary and interdisciplinary. I have used the phrase "Big Idea" with both the universal concepts and disciplinary concepts. For interdisciplinary work and in this book, the term *Big Idea* is used to denote the universal concepts across the curriculum.

Some schools use Big Ideas to plan their entire programs. Plano Independent School District in Texas offers a good example (Allen, 2005). In this district, educators are creating an elementary school that integrates the main subject areas with technology (http://k-12.pisd.edu/currinst/elemen/ic3.htm). Plano develops its lesson plans around these Big Ideas:

- Balance
- Systems
- Communications
- Interactions
- Continuity
- Change
- Diversity

The social studies curriculum as found in the Ontario Ministry of Education (2004), *Social Studies 1* recently identified its Big Ideas—its fundamental and related concepts. This document can be accessed at http://www.edu.gov.on.ca, by following the Ontario Curriculum link. The fundamental concepts are as follows:

- Systems and structures: human patterns, community, cooperation, governance, causation/cause and effect, natural patterns, environment.
- Interactions and interdependence: causation/cause and effect, human and natural patterns, trade exchanges, globalization, community, relationships, civic rights and responsibilities, environment, ecology.
- Environment: human and natural systems, human and natural patterns, exploitation and utilization of resources, regions, ecosystems, urbanization.
- Change and continuity: causation/cause and effect, human and natural systems, human and natural patterns, time, sustainability, tradition, conflict and cooperation.
- Culture: spirituality; ideology; economic, political, and legal systems; communication and language; familial and community structures; education; migration; diversity.
- Power and governance: democracy, security, rights and responsibilities, conflict and cooperation, power relationships.

Although these concepts have been associated with social studies, they are in fact universal concepts, and a quick glance reveals that many of the related concepts fit under more than one fundamental concept. They will all also be found in other subject areas. In Ontario, the other disciplines will soon be undergoing a similar exercise in the next iterations of revised curriculum documents. I expect that this will open a new dialogue since the Big Ideas will probably be similar.

Big Understandings

Beyond the Big Ideas is a still higher level of knowledge. Teachers need to teach to the Big Understandings. The term *Big Understandings* is used in the same sense as an "enduring understandings." An enduring understanding is the knowledge that will endure long past the lesson, for years to come (Wiggins & McTighe, 2005). Big Understandings are also known as *essential learnings* or *generalizations* (Erickson, 2001). Such understandings are similar to Big Ideas because they are broad, abstract, universal in application, and timeless. However, usually a Big Understanding connects two concepts or Big Ideas. They can seem very superficial, but they are actually quite profound in that they express a relationship that is true in many different contexts or cultures.

Big Understandings are not always immediately apparent in curriculum documents. They are easiest to find in the more broad-based standards. Sometimes documents identify the standards that are most important in a topic area, and often, Big Understandings emerge from these standards. Consider the following Big Understandings that emerged from disciplinary standards:

- The use, distribution, and significance of resources are affected by the interaction of humans with physical resources.
- Art reflects and shapes culture.
- Patterns are often revealed through statistical analysis, and they enable prediction.
- Diet affects health, appearance, and performance.

Big Understandings found in single disciplines are often spiraled throughout K to 12. With a broader interpretation, these understandings are also interdisciplinary. Later in this chapter, we will see how Big Understandings can be interpreted using an interdisciplinary lens.

What Is Worth Doing?

As educators wrestle with vast amounts of content, there is a continuing shift to generic skills as most important to learn. Some worry that teaching skills is at the expense of "important" content, but one needs the skills to process the content. These skills do not preclude content; rather, the content is a vehicle for acquiring the skills and vice versa. A *do* is always connected to a *know*, as shown in Figure 3.2.

Terry Whitmell developed a course in Information Technology for Grade 9 students at Peel Board of Education, Ontario. This is an activity-based, process-oriented, project-driven program in which students learn technical knowledge, skills, and values through open-ended problem solving. To teach the skills, she needed to apply content from other subject areas. Her own area of expertise is business studies, so she developed a number of business-oriented activities that teach students computer skills. She found that students could learn sophisticated computer skills when they were engaged in real-world business activities. Because the curriculum was interesting and practical to them, the students were not really aware of, and thus, not frightened off by, the difficulty level of the technological skills. Terry's work in her course shows us how the *do* is connected to the *know*.

In interdisciplinary work, "technology across the curriculum" and "language across the curriculum" are not hollow phrases but reflect complex performance skills that all teachers should teach in their areas. Students might, for example, design, create, and market their own product using language arts, applied technology, and so on. Computers can be used to enhance critical thinking and for a variety of educational purposes such

Figure 3.2   The Interdependency of the *Know* and the *Do*

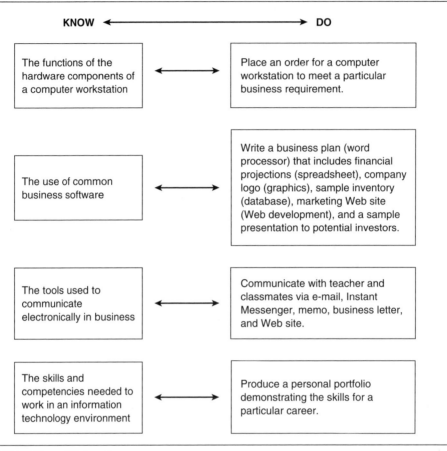

SOURCE: Terry Whitmell.

as experimentation, inquiry, problem solving, interactive learning, drawing, composing, and role playing. Clearly, these uses are not subject or content specific.

Language skills (reading, writing, and listening) are not specific to English classes but rather, apply to all classes. Consider some to the strategies described in *Think Literacy: Cross-Curricular Approaches Grade 7–12* (Ontario Ministry of Education, 2003):

- Reading between the lines (inference)
- Identifying the most and least important ideas in a text
- Drawing conclusions from a text
- Generating ideas for writing
- Webbing and mapping
- Writing a procedure, information report, business report, explanation

- Revising and editing
- Communication strategies (pairs, small groups, whole-class discussions, presentations)

Some teachers are inclined to think that they are a teacher of a subject. "I teach science, not English" has often been the answer to previous attempts to get subject-area teachers to take responsibility for literacy skills. With the new emphasis on literacy, however, a strict disciplinary approach is harder to accept. Many standards in each subject area revolve around communication skills. To be accountable, teachers must teach literacy as it applies to their subjects. Documents such as *Think Literacy: Cross-Curricular Approaches Grade 7–12* (Ontario Ministry of Education, 2003) give teachers the strategies and confidence to teach in areas they may feel are outside their area of expertise. The document is teacher-friendly, describes each skill fully, and offers suggestions for what students can do to practice the skills. Subject-specific versions of *Think Literacy* were released in 2005.

What are the skills that North American graduates must acquire? One view comes from the work-to-school movement. The U.S. Department of Labor (1991) published *What Work Requires of School: A SCANS Report for America 2000,* and in Canada, the Conference Board of Canada (1992) developed the *Employability Skills Profile.* Both documents outline the skills that employers deem necessary for the workplace. These work-related skills are interdisciplinary and not connected to any particular subject area. They include:

- Reading
- Writing
- Basic computation
- Listening
- Speaking
- Creative thinking
- Decision making
- Systems thinking
- Learning how to learn
- Responsibility for self
- Teamwork skills

Inevitably, the *doing* blurs into the *being.* We cannot do something without it being grounded in a value system. In the previous list, arguably only basic computation can be done from a purely objective stance. We read, write, listen, and speak from an often-unrecognized value-laden perspective. Our *doings* are based on a set of values. Systems thinking is embedded in a way of seeing the world. Teamwork and self-responsibility are also value laden. Once again, Terry Whitmell's example in Figure 3.2 can be expanded to show how the KDB are interconnected and interdependent (Figure 3.3).

To further complicate the picture, our students today need to be global citizens. They need sophisticated skills for this role, such as the ability to understand and consider different cultural perspectives and the ability to address issues in different languages. What is worth knowing is not content bound but does involve complex performance skills and is concerned with how we want people to be in the world.

How Do We Want Our Students to Be?

Rarely is *being* identified in the curriculum, although it is usually implicit in the standards. The *being* layer is admittedly problematic because it falls into the territory of values. The controversy revolves around whose values should be taught. Some parents believe that teaching values does not belong in the schools. Some jurisdictions have removed any mention of values from their documents because of public sentiment.

Figure 3.3   The Interdependency of the *Know*, *Do*, and *Be*

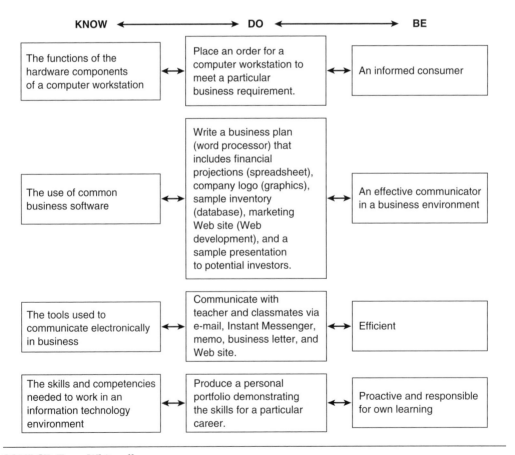

SOURCE: Terry Whitmell.

Some are dealing with values with a revival of character education and service education, which they consider the *be* aspect of the curriculum. Others incorporate values by teaching citizenship.

The reality is that values are taught in the school every day whether we acknowledge it or not. If, for example, the teacher negotiates the curriculum, students experience democratic values. Teachers also have expectations of students that are value laden such as good work habits and respect for others. Many classrooms develop a code of conduct that students follow. These values are the hidden curriculum.

Living in a post–September 11 world, we need to be aware of our values. What are we teaching students to value? I believe it is necessary for us to have conversations, at the very least, about the values we wish to guide curriculum planning. Some schools and districts address this aspect of the curriculum by explicitly naming values that they wish to instill in the students. When one school board in Ontario began to develop student outcomes, it included the community in a meeting held to identify desirable ethical values. Honesty, integrity, trustworthiness, loyalty, fairness, caring, respect, citizenship, pursuit of excellence, and accountability emerged as the desired values for that community.

When we are clear about how we want students to *be*, we can allow these values to guide our curriculum planning. For example, Maximo Microsociety Magnet School in Pinellas County, Florida, follows the life-long guidelines suggested by Kovalik (1994). They are the following:

- Trustworthiness
- Truthfulness
- Active listening
- No put-downs
- Personal best

Expeditionary Learning Outward Bound (2003) builds school culture and fosters character by having a common set of expeditionary learning rituals and traditions stated in its core practices benchmarks. Community meetings, readings, and team-building activities are used in schoolwide activities and in classrooms. Each school develops a set of character traits that teachers constantly focus on and reinforce with students. As well, service learning is integrated with academics.

Service learning is another route to both interdisciplinary work and the *be*. Research on service learning from 1990 to 1999 done by the National Service Learning Partnership indicates that students who engage in service learning demonstrate an increase in the following areas (Billig, 2000):

- Altruism and caring for others
- Concern about their community
- Social competence

- Personal and social responsibility
- Trustworthiness and reliability

Clearly, these characteristics are in the *being* realm. Interestingly, the research also indicated some associated gains in academic skills and knowledge for those who participated in the service learning as well as fewer discipline problems and improved attendance (Billig, 2000).

It is impossible to teach a value-free curriculum unless learning remains at the lowest level of regurgitation of facts. As soon as higher levels of thinking are demanded, students have to apply values. How does one evaluate, process information, problem solve, and apply life skills without some value base? For many teachers, the *be* is actually the most important thing that they teach, and it gives them the greatest rewards.

The Big Picture School Network is an educational reform group that helps design public charter high schools. There are currently 30 such schools around the United States. The network's philosophy stresses that the schools must be personalized and each student must have an equal opportunity to learn. Dennis Littky (2004) of the Met in Providence, Rhode Island, is codirector of the Big Picture Company and plans the curriculum based on what he considers are the real goals for education. He wants students to be:

- Lifelong learners
- Passionate
- Risk takers
- Problem solvers and critical thinkers
- Ingenious thinkers
- Self-directed
- Willing to give back to society
- Creative
- Persevering
- Morally courageous
- Self-respecting
- Able to use the world around them well
- Literate and be able to work with numbers
- Able to truly enjoy life and work

Designing curriculum based on this interpretation of the KDB, students have individualized learning plans that emphasize their unique needs and passions. The curriculum is based on five learning goals that the teachers believe are necessary for success at college and work (Littky, 2004):

- *Communication*—How do I take in and express information?
- *Social reasoning*—What do other people have to say about this?
- *Quantitative reasoning*—How do I measure or represent it?

- *Empirical reasoning*—How do I prove it?
- *Personal qualities*—What do I bring to this process (e.g., respect, honesty, empathy, self-responsibility, perseverance, organization, self-awareness, time management, cooperation, community involvement)?

The Big Picture schools do not teach subjects. These five learning goals are interdisciplinary. They also show how the *know, do,* and *be* are truly interdependent.

THE SCAN AND CLUSTER: USING THE ZOOM LENS TO IDENTIFY THE KDB

The first question of backward design is how to determine what is worth knowing, doing, and being. So far, we have looked at this question with a wide-angle lens. In other words, we looked at what we expected a student to know, do, and be at the end of his or her career as a student. Now we will look at knowing, doing, and being when creating a curriculum at a certain grade level. At this point, we will use a zoom lens to zero in on the mandated standards.

When we are creating a curriculum for a specific level, we need to decide on the *know, do,* and *be* based on the mandated standards for that level. The process begins at the disciplinary level. The KDB Umbrella is the focus for all planning. To identify the KDB at the specific grade level, the standards of each discipline need to be scanned through a "Scan and Cluster" process.

I have developed many curricula with teams of teachers, both as a teacher and as a curriculum professor. In each case, the number of standards we needed to address across selected subject areas overwhelmed us. We found that if we selected broad-based standards representing Big Understandings or Ideas and Big Skills and developed curricula around them, we were actually covering many of the more concrete standards at the same time. This did not mean that we simply checked off a standard when it was peripheral to the core teaching. Rather, we had to teach the smaller standard to authentically cover the broad-based standard.

A Scan and Cluster is done both horizontally and vertically. It is done horizontally to identify patterns across the disciplines. It is also done vertically to identify what the students have learned in the grades before and what is expected in the next grade. If teachers create a curriculum map, a Scan and Cluster is a natural next step (see Chapter 1 for curriculum mapping). This process will take an hour or two but is invaluable for seeing the Big Picture. Once teachers do a Scan and Cluster, they have a new way of thinking about standards. Thereafter, they can easily sweep through the standards to do a Scan and Cluster whenever they need to.

Teachers need an organizer to Scan and Cluster the standards in a relevant manner. A good organizer is using the *know, do,* and *be* categories (Drake & Burns, 2004). With this framework in mind, the first step is the scan. Scanning means skimming all the standards for a general sense of what is required. This gives an overview of the way the KDB Umbrella might be created. The horizontal scan involves scanning across the disciplinary standards for the grade in question. This can be done for the standards of all the disciplines or just the ones that are scheduled for integration. The second scan is to look at the standards vertically for two grades below and one grade above the specific grade level under consideration. This gives a sense of what the students will be expected to know and do and where they are headed in the future.

The process of scanning and clustering can be done on a template similar to a curriculum map, but the map specifically looks at clustering standards from across the curriculum. There are many different ways to do the process. Using colored markers to differentiate between Big Skills and Big Ideas is a very good way to begin. Figure 3.4 offers a horizontal Scan and Cluster, and Figure 3.5 illustrates a vertical Scan and Cluster from the context of the Grade 4 curriculum design on habitats. In Chapter 1, Figure 1.10 also illustrates a vertical Scan and Cluster. A more detailed explanation of scanning and clustering can be found in *Meeting Standards Through Integrated Curriculum* (Drake & Burns, 2004).

Finding the *Know*

Finding the *know* in the documents is done by scanning the different disciplinary documents to identify the Big Ideas or universal concepts. Often, such concepts are poorly identified in the documents. Although this weakness is being addressed in more recent versions of curriculum documents, it is still often up to the educator to determine a conceptual focus to tie the disciplines together. Using interdisciplinary concepts as a lens, educators may scan the grade-level documents and decide that a concept such as "interdependence" is relevant to the standards in more than one subject area. A Grade 4 curriculum, for example, that is integrating content on ecosystems and geographical regions can focus on "interdependence" as a conceptual lens. This allows for a natural connection across the subject areas.

Big Ideas

When scanning for the *know*, it is helpful to keep the structure of knowledge in mind. What are the facts, disciplinary concepts, Big Ideas, and broad-based standards that could serve as Big Understandings? Teachers can identify Big Ideas in curriculum documents by circling or highlighting the nouns that express universal concepts. At this point,

Figure 3.4   A Horizontal Scan and Cluster

Broad-Based Standard	Clusters
Investigate the dependency of plants and animals on their habitat and the interrelationships of the plants and animals living in a specific habitat *(Science)*	*Science* Classify organisms according to their role in the food chain. Demonstrate the understanding of the food chain as a system in which energy from the sun . . . Formulate questions about and identify needs of animals and plants in specific habitat. Use appropriate vocabulary. Compile data through investigation. Construct food chains that include different plant and animal species. *Math* Collect and organize data and identify their use. Predict the results of data collected. Interpret displays of data and present information using mathematical items. Solve simple problems using the concept of probability.
Begin to develop research skills *(English)*	*Social Science* Ask pertinent questions. Locate relevant information. Sort and classify information to identify issues, solve problems, and make decisions. Construct and read a variety of graphs, charts, diagrams, maps, and models. Communicate information using media works, oral presentations, written notes, descriptions, and drawings. Use appropriate vocabulary. *Language Arts* Use vocabulary learned in other subject areas. Use effective openings and closings in oral presentations.
Produce two- or three-dimensional works of art that communicate ideas for specific purposes and to specific audiences *(Visual Art)*	*Visual Art* Identify monochromatic color schemes. Demonstrate awareness that overlapping shapes creates the illusion of depth. Plan a work of art. Solve artistic problems in their art work. Identify strengths and areas of improvement in their own work and others. *Language Arts* Use some vocabulary learned in other subject areas. Use appropriate tone of voice and gestures in social and classroom activities.

SOURCE: Carolyn Bell, Julianne Wiles, and Matthew Lillie.

Figure 3.5   A Vertical Scan and Cluster

	Science	Language Arts	Visual Art	Drama and Dance
Grade 2	Topic: Growth and change in animals Investigate physical and behavioral characteristics and the process of growth of different types of animals.	Communicate ideas for specific purposes. Begin to write more elaborate sentences. Revise and edit work.	Produce 2- and 3-dimensional works of art that communicate ideas or specific purposes.	Communicate understanding of works in drama through discussion, writing, movement, and visual artwork.
Grade 3	Topic: Growth and changes in plants Investigate the requirements of plants and the effects of changes in the environmental conditions on plants.	Communicate ideas for a variety of purposes and specific audiences. Begin to use compound sentences. Revise and edit work.	Produce 2- and 3-dimensional works of art that communicate ideas or specific purposes.	Compare own work with work of others in drama and dance through discussion, writing, movement, and visual artwork.
Grade 4	Topic: Habitats and communities Investigate the dependency of plants and animals on their habitat and the interrelationships of the plants and animals within habitats.	Communicate ideas for a variety of purposes and specific audiences. Begin using complex sentences. Revise and edit work.	Produce 2- and 3-dimensional works of art that communicate ideas or specific purposes.	Communicate orally and in writing response to own and others' work and compare responses.
Grade 5	Topic: Human organ systems Investigate the structure and function of the five major organ systems.	Communicate ideas for a variety of purposes and specific audiences. Use simple, compound, and complex sentences. Revise and edit work.	Produce 2- and 3-dimensional works of art that communicate ideas or specific purposes.	Describe orally and in writing response to own and others' work in drama and dance.

SOURCE: Carolyn Bell, Julianne Wiles, and Matthew Lillie.

teachers can identify the Big Ideas that can act as an umbrella for the disciplines. If there are no Big Ideas embedded into the standards, teachers can add a conceptual focus to bridge the disciplines. Adding a conceptual focus is rarely a false fit; rather, it tends to focus an integrated unit in manageable ways. A conceptual focus that is a natural fit usually is obvious even if it is not stated directly in the documents—since most documents are not yet written from an interdisciplinary perspective.

Erickson's subject area concepts are a good starting place for identifying Big Ideas (Figure 3.6). The list for Big Ideas for social studies on page 48 is also helpful. Some concepts naturally fall into more than one subject area such as "cause and effect" and "interaction." Others such as "time/space," "dynamics," or "ratio" appear in only one subject. Teachers, however, quickly see how most disciplinary concepts can apply to more than one discipline. Deciding whether a Big Idea is in the disciplinary or interdisciplinary realm leads to spirited discussion and a deeper understanding of universal concepts.

Anne Foley (AFoley@umassd.edu) and Marjorie Condon (2005) offer an effective process to determine the Big Ideas. This works for science and social studies or history and geography. Language arts or math standards often represent the process skills needed throughout the teaching of science and social studies. To begin, photocopy all the standards for one subject at a given grade level. Then, cut up the photocopied standards into individual statements, removing any identifying information such as code number or strand (e.g., earth and space science or life systems). Mix up the individual pieces of paper. Sort the standards into piles according to a Big Idea that unites them. There will usually be only three or four piles. Identify an umbrella Big Idea for each pile.

I did this with a group for Grade 1 science and we found that almost every standard fell under the concepts of reproduction, survival, or patterns. These ideas are much bigger than topics such as "bears" or "pioneers." The umbrella for all of our selected three Big Ideas was "interdependence." Similarly, other groups at other grade levels easily completed this process to identify the Big Ideas. Amazingly, the teachers had identified possible themes for a full year. In Chapter 8, there is a sample of a yearlong conceptual map (Figure 8.2). It is not far, then, to connect the Big Ideas across subject areas to create the KDB Umbrella.

Big Understandings

One way to create good Big Understandings is to connect two Big Ideas with a verb (Erickson, 2001). Here are some examples:

- Cultures define conflict.
- Patterns occur in all systems.
- Individual values influence decision making.

Figure 3.6   Examples of Subject-Specific Concepts

Science	Social Studies	Literature
Cause/effect	Cause/effect	Cause/effect
Order	Order	Order
Organism	Patterns	Patterns
Population	Populations	Characters
System	System	Interconnections
Change	Change/culture	Change
Evolution	Evolution	Evolution
Cycle	Cycle	Cycle
Interaction	Interaction	Interaction
Energy matter	Perception	Perception
Equilibrium	Civilization	Intrigue
Field	Migration/immigration	Passion
Force	Interdependence	Hate
Model	Diversity	Love
Time/space	Conflict/cooperation	Family
Theory	Innovation	Conflict/cooperation
Fundamental entities	Beliefs/values	
Replication		
Mathematics	**Visual Art**	**Music**
Number	Rhythm	Rhythm
Ratio	Line	Melody
Proportion	Color	Harmony
Scale	Value	Tone
Symmetry	Shape	Pitch
Probability	Texture	Texture
Pattern	Form	Form
Interaction	Space	Tempo
Cause/effect	Repetition	Dynamics
Order	Balance	Timbre
Quantification	Angle	Pattern
System	Perception	Perception
Theory	Position	
Field	Motion	
Gradient	Light	
Invariance		
Model		

SOURCE: Lynn Erickson, *Stirring the head, heart, and the soul: Redefining curriculum and instruction* (p. 71). Corwin Press. Copyright 1993. Reprinted by permission of the publisher.

Typically, the Big Understanding is connected to the Big Questions. Chapter 5 deals with how to create Big Questions in detail. The same process that is outlined in that chapter can be used for creating Big Understandings.

A logical and common way to identify the Big Understandings is to begin with the disciplinary documents. Are there any standards that stand out as most important for students to meet? Big Understandings are not necessarily immediately apparent in curriculum documents. They are easiest to find in the more broad-based standards. Sometimes documents identify the standards that are most important to learn in a topic area. Usually the Big Understandings emerge from these standards.

Big Understandings found in single disciplines are often spiraled throughout K to 12. With a broader interpretation, these understandings are also interdisciplinary. Figure 3.7 indicates how an understanding that originates from disciplinary standards can be interpreted from an interdisciplinary perspective.

Finding the *Do*

It is important to cluster standards into meaningful chunks to identify the *do*. To find the *do* in disciplinary standards, we need to know (a) what complex performance skills we are looking for, (b) the subset of skills embedded in those complex performance skills, and (c) the criteria necessary to demonstrate the subskills. Most complex skills are found in every disciplinary document. It is very important to have an idea of the skill subset involved in a complex performance skill to be able to cluster skills

Figure 3.7   Interdisciplinary Big Understandings

Big Understanding	Discipline of origin	Related Disciplines
The use, distribution, and significance of resources are affected by the interaction of humans with physical resources.	Geography	Science Mathematics History
Art reflects and shapes culture.	Art	History Geography
Patterns are often revealed through statistical analysis and enable prediction.	Mathematics	History Geography English Science
Diet affects health, appearance, and performance.	Health	Mathematics Science History Geography Physical Education

appropriately. Some of the complex skills one might look for are communication, problem solving, inquiry, design and construction, research and information management, prediction, critical thinking, and presentation skills. These are very big skills that have many parts—all of which may need to be taught.

One helpful method is to use different-colored highlighters to identify the potential standards to chunk together. If, for example, teachers choose research as the skill to be emphasized in an interdisciplinary approach, they would highlight each standard that is related to research in the subject areas. This would include the subset of skills such as asking a question, collecting relevant data, and analyzing the data. We may wish to search for communication skills in a disciplinary document. This is a huge area encompassing reading, writing, listening, and oral language skills. Each set of skills has many subskills within it. Unpacking the standards by noting the verbs will reveal which communication skills are required for each standard.

Within the standards, there is often room for interpretation. When the word *describe* is in a standard, a student must use a communication skill. The description may be demonstrated through writing or speaking. This interpretation is up to the teacher. The student however, is expected, to use language conventions regardless of the method of communication.

Another way to approach the *do* is to look for a smaller skill or subset of skills in the disciplinary guidelines. We may look for "presentation skills" rather than for the larger umbrella of communication skills. Presentation skills will have their own set of criteria that students may need to learn before they can present well.

To scan the documents and cluster them into the *do*, we select a complex skill, identify the subset of skills embedded in it, and recognize the necessary criteria to master the subskills. This sounds very complicated, but once one has done this type of Scan and Cluster, it becomes fairly easy. What makes this task harder is that disciplinary documents generally do not identify the complex skills and the criteria for their sets of subskills explicitly. What makes it vitally important, however, is that the identification of criteria directly aligns with the assessment of interdisciplinary work. These criteria become the performance indicators in the rubrics designed to assess the skills.

Discovering the *Be*

In many standards, the *be* does not exist because they were constructed deliberately to be value free in an effort to avoid the contentious issue of whose values are correct and therefore teachable. Nevertheless, the standards do have implicit values within them. This is particularly true when the standards are broad based.

When doing a Scan and Cluster, teachers can identify the *be* element that is inherent in existing standards. They can analyze the standards to discover implicit values (see Figure 1.5). Also, there is a way to discover the *be* that is implicit in a Big Understanding. The formula is this: "When you understand that (fill in the Big Understanding here), then . . ." This resulting statement identifies the "so what" implicit in a standard and informs us how we want students to *be* in the world.

Figure 3.8 shows how this might look using the Big Understandings that previously may have seemed value free. I am indebted to Nina Schliklin, superintendent of School Union 29, Poland, Maine, for sharing this valuable idea with me.

In this chapter, the characteristics of standard-based curriculum were reviewed. The components of backward design were presented. The first question of backward design was explored from an interdisciplinary perspective. What is worth knowing, doing, and being? The interconnected relationship of the *know, do*, and *be* was explored. Finally, the KDB Umbrella was offered as a way to view the disciplines from a wide-angle lens.

If you have not done so yet, please note that you would be wisest to choose a relevant grade level and set of standards and use them for all the activities in the following chapters.

Figure 3.8   Finding the *Be* in the Big Understandings

When you understand that . . . (Big Understanding)	THEN . . . (BE)
WYUT . . . the earth's water systems influence the climate and weather of the region where they are located.	Then we must use water in a responsible way.
WYUT . . . different geographical regions are interdependent (e.g., economic, cultural, government).	Then we must consider many different aspects of a region and how it affects other regions when making decisions.
WYUT . . . medieval society influenced modern society.	Then we need to study history to understand how the past affects the present so that we can make wise decisions about the future.
WYUT . . . the proper knowledge and use of vocabulary and language conventions affects effective communication.	Then we need to know and use proper language conventions so that we can communicate effectively with others and so that we can succeed in life.
WYUT . . . the human use of technology has an impact on ecosystems. Humans are responsible to preserve ecosystems.	Then we must use technology in a way that sustains ecosystems.

NOTE: WYUT = When you understand that . . .

DISCUSSION QUESTIONS

1. Explain what the structure of knowledge means to you.

2. How are the *know, do*, and *be* connected? Give an example in your own context of this relationship.

3. Read about Big Ideas and Big Understandings (*know*) and Big Skills (*do*). Discuss how this view of what is most important to learn shifts how you design curriculum.

4. How do feel about the inclusion of the *be* as most important to learn? How might you teach the *be*?

SUGGESTED ACTIVITIES

1. Select standards in three or four subject areas. Include social studies (history/geography) and science. Identify the Big Ideas and Big Understandings, recognizing that the curriculum may or may not do it for you. Figure 3.4, Figure 3.5, and Figure 3.6 should be useful to you.

2. Read about the *do*. Using the same standards as in the previous question, identify the Big Skills. Remember that the Big Skills are not necessarily identified for you. You need to scan the standards to see what Big Skills are embedded in the standards. Some Big Skills would be communication (e.g., writing, presentation), problem solving, critical thinking, and design and construction. Then you must look for the subset of skills of the Big Skill. For example, some of the subset skills for research are found in Figure 1.8.

3. Choose several broad-based standards (from different subject areas). Using the formula from Figure 3.8, extrapolate to discover the *be* in the standard.

4. Perform a Scan and Cluster of the standards for your desired grade level. See Figure 3.4 for an example of a horizontal scan and Figures 1.10, 3.5 to see examples of a vertical scan. Begin with a horizontal scan (across the desired grade level) of the standards in the desired subject areas. Using different-colored highlighters, scan one curriculum document at a time to identify the *know, do*, and *be*. When you have completed that task, do a vertical scan (two grades below and one grade above). What patterns do you see?

4

How Do Teachers Know When Students Have Met Expectations?

The previous chapter explored the first question of backward mapping: What should students know, do, and be? This chapter examines the second question of backward mapping: How do we, as teachers, know when students know it? What evidence do we have of their knowledge and understanding? What criteria will determine levels of performance?

Before addressing this second question, this chapter explores interdisciplinary assessment: What is it? How do you do it? Who does it? What is assessed? This is followed by an exploration of ways to create substantive Big Assessment tasks (interdisciplinary core assessment tasks) that are aligned with the Know/Do/Be (KDB) Umbrella. Finally, we look at appropriate assessment tools to measure levels of student performance on the Big Assessment task.

INTERDISCIPLINARY ASSESSMENT

What Is It?

The term *interdisciplinary assessment* describes the assessment of concepts and skills that cut across the curriculum—the *know* (Big Understandings and

Ideas), the *do* (Big Skills), and the *be*. The teacher can assess more than one subject at a time. To think about assessment from an interdisciplinary perspective, one must view the curriculum from the Big Picture perspective.

Although a test is fine as one type of evaluation tool, interdisciplinary assessment tasks require much more. Students must show what they know through what they do. Assessment tasks are performance based and, as a result, look much like a rich instructional activity. However, the assessment is embedded in the instructional strategy and needs to be aligned with the KDB. Appropriate assessment tools need to accompany the rich assessment tasks; these tools measure the level of student accomplishment on the learning goals during that activity.

Integrated assessment raises some confusing issues. Usually, teachers must report student achievement in a specific discipline. Indeed, students need to attain disciplinary standards. Naturally, then, teachers tend to think in disciplinary blocks. However, when they shift from the disciplinary focus to the Big Picture, they can work differently. In fact, many teachers say the only way they can assess everything is to integrate the curriculum!

Interdisciplinary assessment is not a term that is frequently used. Yet much of the assessment done in the disciplines can be used in an interdisciplinary way. Big Understandings and Ideas are universal and timeless, cutting across the disciplines. (A review of Figure 3.7 shows how a seemingly disciplinary understanding can be truly interdisciplinary.) Thus, in each subject, students are studying Big Understandings and Ideas that could also be explored in other subject areas.

The Big Skills are also interdisciplinary. They are complex, require the acquisition of a subset of skills, and are embedded in the standards. For example, every discipline requires some communication skills. Communication skills should not fall simply into the realm of English or language arts. They rightfully belong in every subject. They are life skills that everyone needs to be successful. Research skills are also found in every subject. They may have a slightly different slant, but basically, research is research. This is the same with most of the Big Skills.

The *be* is always interdisciplinary. It is about how a student undertakes a task—what he or she does with the *know* and *do*. The *be* is not always assessed. Many districts include the *be* in an anecdotal report or as a checklist. Teaches may choose, for example, to assess the effort a student has put into a project or how he or she cooperated in a group. The *be* is often a separate category on the rubric and, in turn, on the report card. In Ontario, the *be* is reported at the secondary level as a learning skills checklist of characteristics such as independent work, initiative, teamwork skills, ability to organize, and homework and work habits. The report for elementary students is similar but includes cooperation with others, conflict resolution, problem solving and class participation, cooperation, independence, and ability to resolve conflict. Unfortunately, the learning skills are generally not as highly valued as the grades in subject areas, although many teachers believe they should be.

To state the most obvious, the *know* (content) of interdisciplinary assessment tasks comes from more than one subject area. The *do* of most assessment tasks, even when they are subject based, is already interdisciplinary. We see this in cross-curricular skills such as writing or research skills. When a student gives a PowerPoint presentation about American foreign policy in his history class, he is using a skill set that is equally applicable to his success in an English presentation on Jane Austen's social criticism. It is just as important for academic success to learn the interdisciplinary skills as it is to acquire the mandated knowledge of a subject. It is the use of the assessment task, not the task itself, that determines whether it is disciplinary or interdisciplinary.

From the Big Picture perspective, all assessment tasks are generic. The teacher has a wide range of choices—but it is not an infinite list. Some tasks are more complex than others, and thus different tasks are more appropriate in different situations. Some assessment tasks are listed in Figure 4.1.

Assessment *Of*, *For*, and *As* Learning

Teachers also need to think of the purpose for the assessment. Earl (2003) differentiates among assessment *of* learning (summative), assessment *for* learning (diagnostic and formative), and assessment *as* learning (promotes student learning). Summative evaluation is given at the end point of an instructional segment and is intended to sum up what a student has learned. Traditionally, summative assessment is a test, and it has its place in any educational system. However, a summative assessment can also be a performance assessment that can be interdisciplinary and include the KDB. At the Met, students give exhibitions as their summative evaluation (Littky, 2004). These exhibitions are conversations in which the students talk about the process of their learning (*do*), and they emphasize both personal growth (*be*) and the depth of their learning (*know*). Also, students set high standards for themselves (*be*) and develop action plans for what comes next (assessment as learning).

The November 2005 issue of *Educational Leadership* is a theme issue on "Assessment to Promote Learning" and is an excellent resource on how to implement both assessment for and as learning. Shifting to these types of assessments results in significant increases in student test scores and in student learning (Black, Harrison, Lee, Marshall, & Wiliam, 2003). It also requires a dramatic shift in most teachers' practices. Assessment *for* learning includes diagnostic assessment that allows the teacher to make decisions on the direction the teaching should go. Often, this type of assessment is given at the beginning of a unit. Formative assessment is ongoing feedback that enables the students to improve at the same time as

Figure 4.1   A Sampling of Assessment Tasks

Sample Assessment Tasks			
Big Book	Survey	Videotape	Song
Crafts	Attendance	Report	Interviews
Flow Chart	Election	Brochure	Editorial
Musical Instrument	Participation in Discussion	Play an Instrument	Persuasive Writing
Voluntary Responses	Research Project/Paper	Architectural Design	Computer Program
Puppets	Sculpture	Menu	Eulogy
Map	Family Tree	Mobile	Painting
Recipe	Timeline	Scale Model	Flag
Fiction	Panel Discussion	Costume	Collage
Coordinate an Event	Advertisement, Commercial	Design and Build a Model	Musical Composition
Invention	Constitution	Pantomime	Play Set
Multimedia Presentation	Newspaper, Magazine	Film - Movie Documentary	Instructions, Guidebook
Slide Show	News Story	Diorama	Mock Trial
Jewelry	Teamwork	Debates	Dance
Poetry	Experiments	Visual Display	Photo Essay

it informs the teacher. Students act as active assessors in the assessment *as* learning process. Students assess their own work. Assessment as learning may include journaling, self-assessment, peer assessment, portfolios, and student/teacher/parent conferencing. All tasks require that the learner be reflective about his or her learning. The line between formative assessment and assessment *as* learning is often believed.

What Are Interdisciplinary Assessment Tools?

Interdisciplinary assessment tools accompany an interdisciplinary assessment task and are used to measure levels of achievement. They, too, are generic. Again, it is the use of the tool that determines if it is interdisciplinary or not. These are some interdisciplinary assessment tools:

- Checklists
- Rubrics
- Classroom tests
- Maps
- Self-assessments
- Peer assessments
- Graphic organizers
- Concept maps
- Portfolios
- Conferences

Both the task and the tool can be adapted to certain circumstances. A generic assessment tool can be applied to each generic product. An advertisement is an advertisement, for example, regardless of the nature of the subject. This is true for any number of generic products such as newspaper articles, persuasive writing, and a brochure. Each product meets certain criteria to be acceptable. One can create an assessment tool based on these criteria, rather than on the characteristics of a discipline. The Curry-Samara model (www.curriculumproject.com), which will be further explored in Chapter 7, illustrates this important concept. Curry and Samara have developed many templates for generic products that students may do as assessment tasks. For this book, Curry and Samara share an example of a timeline (Figure 7.4).

Who Is Responsible for Teaching the Cross-Curricular Skills?

The "Big Picture teacher" needs to accept responsibility for teaching the procedural skills or making sure students learn the skills necessary to perform the assessment task he or she is asking for. For example, if the students are required to create a computer-generated brochure, they will need to be taught how to manipulate the software to do so. Thus, the teacher needs to have an understanding of the skill to teach and assess it effectively. This may mean a willingness to learn a new skill.

Students can't be expected to demonstrate what they do not know how to do. I learned this lesson many years ago. Bruce Hemphill, Ron Chappell, and I were teaching a Grade 9 integrated curriculum. Our students had developed final presentations for their culminating activity. We were thrilled with the students' learning. Confident that others would also be impressed, and hoping to convert our audience to interdisciplinary approaches, we had asked other teachers and parents to attend the presentations. But at the event, the students' presentations were dreadful. The students mumbled into their cheat sheets. Our last hope of redemption lay with a young woman who came to the stage with an audiotape. Alas, she simply turned on the tape recorder and sat there while it played, her barely audible voice whispering her words. After that, we always taught presentation skills before we asked students to perform. Also, we assessed these skills to show the students that we believed they were very important.

Who Assesses What?

Judy Sara is an interdisciplinary curriculum coordinator who spent time studying interdisciplinary assessment as a research project for her master's of education degree. She teaches at the Australian Science and Mathematics School in Adelaide, Australia. This school was set up in 2002 to lead the reform in science and mathematics. It offers an innovative program designed to integrate technology across the curriculum. Although Judy's examples are in the area of nanotechnology, they are really informative for anyone doing interdisciplinary work with any subjects at any level.

Under the title "Toward Nanotechnology," Judy and a group of eight other teachers implemented an 18-week program of 500 minutes weekly for Grade 11 in nanotechnology. There are 12 summative assessments in her program. Judy and her team discovered that they were confronted with assessment tasks outside their areas of expertise. For Judy, coping with this reality is often a question of attitude and willingness to learn new things. What is the purpose of teaching students the skills to be a lifelong learner if teachers believe that the only things they can do are ones they learned while studying to be a teacher at a university? In her experience— and she attended a faculty of education 30 years ago—teachers can learn new things and are more than capable of teaching and assessing in areas other than their university-trained specialization.

Judy and her colleagues came to recognize that there were many ways to assess interdisciplinary work effectively. One way to assess is to have different teachers from different subject areas evaluate their subject-specific part of an assessment task. In the unit called "Technological World," the teachers assessed more than one subject in a number of tasks. For example, students worked in groups of three on the fertile question: "What technology has had the most significant impact on society?" This task was assessed as a science or history task as well as an English task. The groups selected a particular technology and researched it. Then, students each wrote an essay on the impact of their chosen technology on society based on either the science behind the chosen technology or the history of it. This task had English, technology, science, and history rubrics attached to it. The English teacher marked all the essays; the science teacher marked the science and technology essays; a history specialist marked the history essays. In this way, each teacher had a "grade" for reporting in his or her respective discipline.

In another approach, teachers may focus the assessment on only one subject area, although they rely on other subject areas to complete the task. In "Toward Nanotechnology," the Australian team made the decision to concentrate the assessment tasks on only one subject area—even though they were using information that came from a number of areas. The Big Assessment task that serves as an example later in this chapter follows this tradition. The Big Assessment task was used to assess English but relied on knowledge from one of the main culminating tasks—a Nano Innovation Expo. An English and a science specialist jointly designed the task. All the teachers assessed the results of this task. A number of the teachers on the team had not taught English before. The English specialist enlightened them on terminology such as "register" and "form." She gave them examples of what to look for and tips for teaching. Also, she showed them examples of the types of comments she would put on different papers and gave feedback on their comments. The English teachers also taught and assessed this task. They relied on the science teacher's expertise to judge the validity of the science and technology that the students were bringing to the town meeting. This is an excellent example of how literacy across the curriculum can be implemented.

In yet another approach, teachers, peers, invited students, and the invited guests were asked to contribute to the evaluation of the culminating Big Assessment task for the Nano Innovation Expo. Students designed nanoproducts and displayed their ideas such as stopping the spread of cancer, portable thin TV screens, paints to make planes fly faster, and medicine delivered on contact lenses. The nanoproduct was assessed primarily as a science task, but it also brought in skills from English and philosophy. Visitors received a comprehensive assessment tool that included a description of the task and several rubrics to assess the level of achievement for presentation of the product, rationale for developing the product, the ability to explain the science behind the rubric, a detailed explanation of how the product would be manufactured, and their confidence in this product as a good financial investment. This task and assessment tool can be found as a Webquest under http://curriculum.asms.flinders.edu.au/nano/index.html. The assessment booklet can be downloaded from the teachers' page.

For Judy Sara and her team, there are many similarities regardless of what approach is chosen to evaluate interdisciplinary work. Teachers decide what they want the students to know and do for each assessment task. Then they spend time developing, reviewing, and revising rubrics according to teacher and student responses. For example, the team has revised the rubrics to have five levels of performance rather than the traditional four. Many students perform very well but do not meet the extremely high criteria that the teachers tend to set for the highest level. The teachers found they could measure a truly exemplary performance if five categories were available.

How do teachers assign disciplinary grades from interdisciplinary tasks? Often this is straightforward once a teacher has selected certain standards from different disciplines. The task may result in grades for different subject areas. Melissa Rubocki of District School Board of Niagara has developed her own method (Drake & Burns, 2004). She keeps a record of each standard in each subject area. When a student completes a standard in one subject area, she assigns a level on that standard and records it in her mark book. In this way, she can actually assess standards from any number of subject areas at one time. When she needs to grade the students, she takes into consideration both the levels they acquired for each standard across one subject area and the difficulty or complexity of the standard. She then translates this into a letter grade as required in Ontario for elementary students.

A SAMPLE OF A BIG ASSESSMENT TASK

Creating a Big Assessment task requires thoughtful reflection. Students should be given a written copy of the task early—perhaps on the first day of the unit. The task should be written in the active voice and in the present tense. The KDB, the context, the students' role, and the audience need to be clearly stated. Finally, the product or performance should be described fully with a detailed explanation of the criteria for assessment.

The following interdisciplinary core assessment task from Judy Sara's team in its "Toward Nanotechnology" unit serves as a good example. I have created the KDB Umbrella (Figure 4.2) below on the basis of their work. The goal of the unit was to demonstrate both knowledge of (*know*) and the ability to use (*do*) the function and power of language. The English component was the only subject assessed, as the team already had enough assessments for science.

Students used their knowledge of nanotechnology to demonstrate the language skills of choosing words and language for specific purposes;

Figure 4.2   A Know/Do/Be Umbrella for a "Toward Nanotechnology" Big Assessment Task

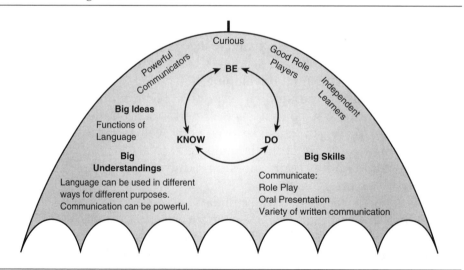

SOURCE: Based on the work of the Australian Science and Mathematics School curriculum writers.

they were required to reflect on a previous assessment task—the Nano Innovation Expo. Students also had to demonstrate a good grasp of the science content to fulfill the language expectations. Also, they were expected to be innovative problem solvers, good team members, and good role players during this time (*be*). Table 4.1 afters the Big Assessment task, and Figure 4.3 show the rubric that accompanies the task.

PLANNING BIG ASSESSMENT TASKS

When curriculum designers plan backward, they need to "think like assessors" (Wiggins & McTighe, 2005). Similarly, when planning integrated curriculum, educators need to think like "interdisciplinary assessors." This means that educators are not simply designing engaging activities for students. They design with assessment as a priority. The key to a relevant interdisciplinary curriculum is a relevant and challenging Big Assessment task. The learning activities leading to the Big Assessment task will need to be relevant and challenging. It is not enough to experience a field trip, for example. The field trip is a part of a Big Assessment task because it contributes to the students' learning of content and skills that, in turn, result in a complex assessment task that aligns with the KDB.

As interdisciplinary assessors, the teachers need to address three questions as they create their assessment tasks. At all times, they are focusing on the KDB Umbrella.

Table 4.1   A Big Assessment Task for "Toward Nanotechnology"

Big Assessment Task

The Scenario

There are plans to build a nanotech factory at Pt. Cimota, a town that is undergoing economic decline and needs new industry. Several problematic issues have emerged including the safety of the new technology. The goal of the town council meeting is to reach an agreement about how to solve the problems and to produce a signed statement committing every member to a specific action in response to the issues including the acceptance or rejection for building the nanofactory.

The Context

You are a member of the town council who has been assigned a specific role to play. Your role will be decided by a "lucky dip" from a container. There will be several of you playing the same role because there are a number of town councils within the class. This group of members playing the same role will constitute your planning group. You will meet in your planning group to discuss how you might play the character in role and what issues the character might raise. As well, you need to decide what types of words the character may use and how he or she might act.

(Continued)

Table 4.1 (Continued)

Now you will join your town council group. The members of the council are:

1. Dr. Serious, the Mayor for PT Bin

2. A scientific advisor from Madlab University

3. A member of the Pt. Cimota EnviroCare group

4. The manager of the Gizmo & Co. Productions factory

5. An unemployed person

6. A local window cleaner/supermarket employee

7. A local shopkeeper

Under the chairpersonship of Dr. Serious, your group:

❑   Uses a tape recorder to tape the meeting
❑   Selects a scribe to record group discussions and recommendations
❑   Conducts the meeting with the mayor as chairperson for the group discussion
❑   Selects a spokesperson for debriefing session

The mayor also needs to be prepared to open the town council meeting with a speech.

The Activity

1. You play your role at the town council meeting and address the issues that arise.
2. At a debriefing session, the selected member of your group presents your group's recommendations to the whole class.
3. You will write a number of newspaper articles for the local paper about the Pt. Cimota nanoplant. Your articles will discuss the main points of discussion of your council meeting, the final agreed statement about Pt. Cimota, and a description about how the different councillors acted at the meeting.

Assessment Task

Prepare a section of the newspaper. It will contain at least three articles and at least two visuals.

Article 1: Provide an outline of the group discussions on building the nanofactory. This may include:

❑   Worthwhile information from any role-play group at the debriefing session
❑   The recommendation of the group
❑   Your opinion of recommendations as a journalist for a local newspaper
❑   Emphasis on the function and power of language
❑   A minimum of two visuals

Article 2: Describe how different individuals communicated at the meeting.

Article 3: Include:

❑   A reflection of the nanoproduct you developed
❑   How the group worked
❑   Why the group decided on a certain nanoproduct
❑   How you found out about science and fabrication
❑   Feedback from the assessors

You will be assessed on the function and power of language, the drafting process, as well as language conventions. The power of your communication will depend on your accurate knowledge of nanotechnology.

SOURCE: Australian Science and Mathematics School Curriculum

Step 1: What do I need to know before I can create a Big Assessment task?

　(a) What is the KDB? What are the generic criteria necessary to demonstrate the KDB?

　(b) What are the broad-based standards that the KDB represents?

　(c) What are the possible activities and assessments embedded in the standards?

Step 2: What kind of assessment task (evidence) do we need to show the KDB?

Step 3: What assessment tools can we use to measure the evidence and provide specific criteria to distinguish levels of performance?

Step 1: What Do I Need to Know Before I Can Create a Big Assessment Task?

(a) What Is the KDB? What Are the Generic Criteria Necessary to Demonstrate the KDB?

This may look like two separate questions, but they are actually two sides of the same coin. When teachers work with interdisciplinary assessment, they need to have an idea of the fundamental makeup of the Big Understandings/Ideas and Big Skills first. Recognizing these fundamentals in the existing documents is the only way that they will be able to identify the KDB and create the KDB Umbrella.

The basic assumption is that the *know* and the *do* are embedded into every curriculum document from K to 12. These Big Understandings/Ideas and Big Skills spiral through the curriculum so a student is meeting them again and again in an increasingly sophisticated way. I saw this as I selected examples for this book. At Grades 4, 7, 9, and 10, the teachers were expected to teach "systems" and "interdependence" and that "humans have an impact on the environment." At every grade level, teachers were expected to teach problem solving, literacy, and research skills among other things. Yet every curriculum was very different, particularly when it was set in its local context. Similarly, the same type of assessment tasks and accompanying tools appeared at every grade level. Armed with this understanding, teachers can Scan and Cluster for these interdisciplinary criteria (subskills) in the documents. They can create effective curriculum maps looking for natural connections as described in Chapter 1 (see Figures 1.9 to 1.12).

Given that the *know* and *do* are embedded in the documents, the teachers need to be able to find them. They may not find the *know* or *do* in its entirety, but they may, for example, find some of the subskills of a Big Skill embedded in the standards. The subskills are the criteria for the

Figure 4.3   The Rubric for a "Toward Nanotechnology" Big Assessment Task

Www.asms.sa.au   Your Name_____

Toward Nanotechnology
The Function and Power of Language
Awareness of **features and functions** of language.
Accuracy and fluency of expression in an appropriate **form and register.**

	Beginning 1	Development 2	Proficient 3	Accomplished 4	Exemplary 5
Drafting Process	Draft of one article handed in.	Drafts of some articles presented and some feedback acted upon.	Drafts of all 3 articles and newspaper pages presented and some feedback acted upon.	Drafts of all 3 articles and newspaper articles presented a number of times and some feedback acted upon.	Drafts of all 3 articles and newspaper pages presented a number of times. Each draft shows considerable improvement.
Word Choice	Writer struggles with a limited vocabulary, groping for words to convey meaning.	Often language is vague and abstract or does not contain enough detail. Some incorrect concepts.	Words are chosen adequately to describe activities and show reflection.	Sense of writing flair with challenging use of words. Imagery identified.	Words convey the intended message in an interesting, precise, and natural way. The writing is full and rich, yet concise.
Accuracy	Sequence is difficult to follow. Lacking a central idea or focus.	Ideas are haphazard, mechanical with occasional awkward construction.	An easy flow where ideas are easy to follow.	Information in logical sequence. Sentences well built with consistently strong and varied structure.	Information is logical, interesting sequence with sections built around sound topic sentences.
Format and Register Fluency of Expression	No clear understanding is evident.	Need to look at ways to change language to suit the audience.	Clear understanding of the appropriate choices of language for a presentation.	Multiple examples and references used or explained. Evidence of a variety of registers to suit audience and purpose.	Language used is innovative and register is most appropriate for the audience.

SOURCE: Australian Science and Mathematics School curriculum writers.

Big Skill. For example, teachers will recognize that when a standard requires a student to develop a good question, this is the first step in research. Asking a good question is a subskill for the Big Skill of research, as well as a skill in its own right. Asking a good question does not belong to one discipline. On the contrary, it is necessary for all subject areas.

This means that a prerequisite for thinking like an interdisciplinary assessor is to have a working familiarity with the characteristics of the Big Understandings/Ideas and Big Skills. It is a bit of a chicken-and-egg dilemma. How do teachers learn the criteria for the KDB? Do teachers need to learn them before they start curriculum mapping or before they do a Scan and Cluster? Will teachers learn the criteria naturally as they work with generic assessment tools and those curriculum documents that show the spiraling of concepts and skills for each strand in a subject? Or are descriptions of the criteria in a state of ongoing development as a group of teachers make sense of them in their context?

I think it is a bit of each. As with anything else, teachers' knowledge of criteria for the KDB will deepen as they get more experience and reflect on this experience.

(b) What Are the Broad-Based Standards That the KDB Represents?

A good way to connect the mandated curriculum and the assessment to the KDB Umbrella is to choose two or three broad-based standards to represent the desired learning. These standards may come from all the subjects involved in the integration, or they may represent just one subject. This often happens when the standards are very similar in two subject areas such as science and geography or when the integrating subjects such as English or math are being used as process skills. A broad-based standard is one that is global in nature, and many examples may sit under its umbrella. In this sense, it is similar to Big Understandings/Ideas. In fact, as we have already seen, Big Understandings sometimes come directly from the broad-based standards.

An important characteristic of a broad-based standard is that many more concrete standards fall under it. This is how teachers can incorporate many standards when they cover a broad-based one. Examples of broad-based standards are the following:

Students will:

- Understand the three states of matter and of changes in those states.
- Use a variety of strategies to help them read.
- Apply numeracy skills in everyday situations using concrete objects.
- Use multiple approaches to exploring and inquiring.
- Demonstrate responsible emotional and cognitive behaviors.

(c) What Are the Possible Activities and Assessments Embedded in the Standards?

In the act of creating the KDB, teachers also need to have some idea of the kind of activities and assessments that are suggested by the standards. This requires two-dimensional thinking again. To do this, it is helpful to develop an exploratory web. In this way, teachers can look at the standards in the different subject areas and see what kinds of activities are suggested by the standards in each area. Often this leads to activities and assessments that are interdisciplinary. It is important that this web is exploratory because it may change drastically as the curriculum designers move forward. A template for an exploratory web is in Figure 4.4.

Step 2: What Kind of Big Assessment Task (Evidence) Do We Need to Demonstrate the KDB?

What Big Assessment task will offer the best evidence to show student achievement of the KDB? In backward mapping, Wiggins and McTighe (2005) refer to core assessment tasks. These are complex assessment tasks that get at the heart of the learning. A Big Assessment task is a core assessment task. It may be a culminating activity that ends the unit and acts as a summative evaluation. In a longer unit, there may be more than one Big Assessment task. Also, a unit may include some core assessment tasks that are disciplinary but set in the context of the broader KDB Umbrella.

The Big Assessment task must be comprehensive, multidimensional, and interdisciplinary. The *know* and the *do* in the task are embedded in the standards across the disciplines. Thus, the student is reaching the standards in more than one discipline through one assessment task. The students of Terry Whitmell, whom you met in Chapter 3, learned technological skills (*do*) using the *know* of business studies. Their culminating assessment task was to create a business plan. To do so, students had to use their technological skills. Terry also expected them to *be* informed consumers; efficient, effective communicators; and responsible for their own learning (see Figure 3.3).

The *know* is often derived from science and social studies. English and math offer process skills. Also, the arts often act as process skills. Students can demonstrate what they know through the creation of a piece of art. It is important again to ensure that the process skills are taught! A visual arts teacher, for example, needs to know that the integrity of his or her discipline is intact when students create an art piece to demonstrate their knowledge in science.

A review of Figure 4.1 shows a variety of potential assessment tasks. A Big Assessment task may include one or more of them. This depends on the complexity of the task and the KDB Umbrella.

Figure 4.4   An Exploratory Web

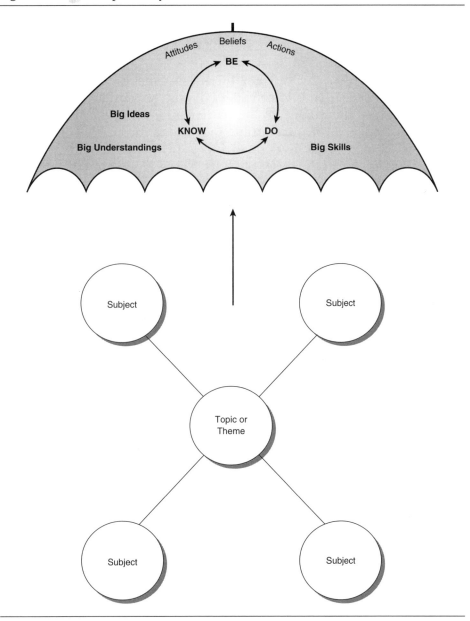

Step 3: What Assessment Tools Can We Use to Measure the Evidence and Provide Specific Criteria to Distinguish Levels of Performance?

Once the assessment task is determined, an appropriate tool is selected or created to measure student success at the task. Because a Big Assessment task is complex, more than one assessment tool may be needed to articulate expectations of success in various components. For example, an assessment tool for a Big Assessment task may include the teacher's observations, a checklist for participation in a class discussion, and a rubric that outlines the criteria for the task and measures levels of performance. Regardless of its sophistication, any assessment tool needs to articulate the criteria for success. If it is a checklist for participation, for example, the teacher needs to consider not only how often a student participates but also the quality of the participation. If it is a dance that is being evaluated, a rubric can outline the criteria for an effective performance including a carefully defined subset of skills. Also, there will be levels of success for each subset of skills. These levels are the categories for rubrics—traditionally four categories are used ranging from a poor performance to an excellent one.

It is also important that whatever tool is used, it is of high quality— one that measures what it is supposed to measure with validity, reliability, and consistency. This is murky territory, and teachers need a lot of training to create high-quality assessments. Although there are some fine examples of assessment tools available on the Internet, many are poorly constructed. Discussion among teachers about the quality of assessment tools builds assessment literacy. As well, the process of doing a Scan and Cluster and developing the KDB Umbrella helps build a better understanding of assessment.

HOW SOME TEACHERS PLANNED THE BIG ASSESSMENT TASK

Tom Martin, John Molnar, and Phil Teeuwsen developed an interdisciplinary "Habitat" unit for Grade 4 students. They followed the three basic steps for creating a Big Assessment task. We will follow them through their process.

Step 1: What Do I Need to Know Before I Can Create a Big Assessment Task?

(a) What Is the KDB? What Are the Generic Criteria Necessary to Demonstrate the KDB?

What are the criteria that demonstrate the KDB? Armed with some knowledge of what Big Understandings/Ideas and Big Skills look like, these teachers did a Scan and Cluster of the standards in science, language arts, visual arts, and drama and dance. They created a horizontal Scan and Cluster and a vertical Scan and Cluster (please refer back to Figures 3.4 and 3.5). With this information, they proceeded to create the KDB Umbrella. The KDB Umbrella is in Figure 4.5.

(b) What Are the Broad-Based Standards
That the KDB Represents?

To identify the KDB was not a difficult task. The Ontario's overall Grade 4 science expectations (www.edu.gov.on.ca) guided their work. They focused heavily on science for the *know* of the curriculum, and the Big Understandings/Big Ideas were easily identified within the standards (expectations) themselves. They selected the following overall or broad-based expectations:

Figure 4.5   A Know/Do/Be Umbrella for "Habitats"

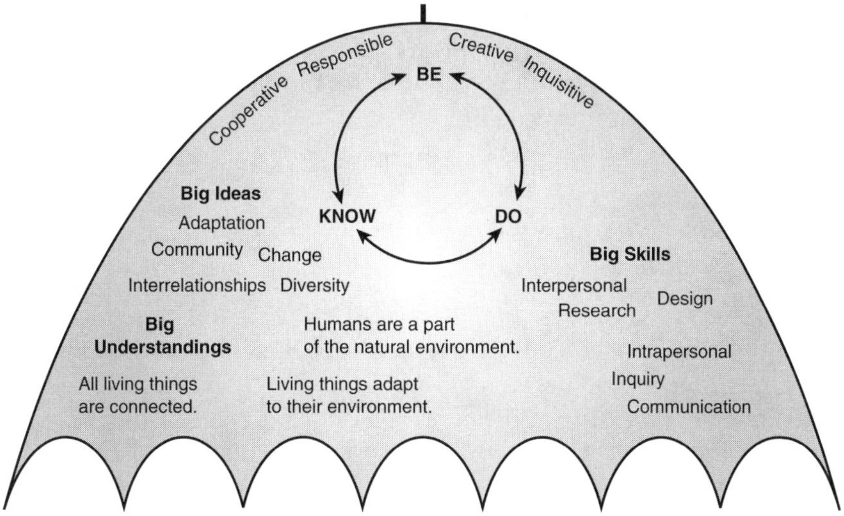

SOURCE: Based on the work of Tom Martin, Phil Teeuwsen, and John Molnar.

- Demonstrate an understanding of the concepts of habitats and community, and identify factors that affect habitats and communities of plants and animals.
- Investigate the dependency of plants and animals on their habitat and the interrelationships of the plants and animals living in a specific habitat.
- Describe ways in which humans can change habitats and the effects of these habitats on the plants and animals within the habitat.

Although the core content was science based, this was an interdisciplinary unit that included math, language arts, drama, social studies, science, and visual arts. The *do* skills cut across the disciplines. The problem solving revolved around an experiment required in the science curriculum. The research belonged in language arts. Different methods of communication were involved in all subject areas. Drama was derived from the arts. Mapping came from social sciences. Above all, they wanted students to be cooperative, responsible for their own behavior, creative, and inquisitive. Once they had done this, they created their KDB Umbrella as seen in Figure 4.5.

(c) What Are the Possible Activities and Assessments Embedded in the Standards?

Before Tom, Phil, and John did theirs can and Cluster, they discussed the Grade 4 curriculum. They were experienced teachers who had the advantage of knowing the curriculum, and each had a good sense of what was important to teach. They had a good understanding of the fundamental makeup of the Big Skills and were familiar with the concepts they needed to teach in Grade 4. This allowed them to go through the Scan and Cluster process relatively quickly to find the Big Ideas and Big Skills. They used broad-based standards as Big Understandings. They found the criteria for the skills embedded in the standards.

(d) Are There Any Possible Activities Embedded in the Standards?

To explore possibilities for their curriculum unit, they created an exploratory web. This web looked at standards in different subject areas that could be included in the unit as and integrated activities assessments. This exploration also gave them a good sense of what type of Big Assessment task could be aligned with the discipline-specific standards. Their web is in Figure 4.6.

Step 2: What Kind of Assessment Task (Evidence) Do We Need to Demonstrate the KDB?

Now they were ready to develop their Big Assessment task that would act as a culminating activity (see Table 4.2).

This was a straightforward interdisciplinary core assessment task directly connected to the broad-based standards. The authors needed to constantly check that the task was aligned with their KDB Umbrella. It focused directly on the Big Understandings and Ideas. The Big Skills were interdisciplinary. The *be* would be evident while the students prepared for the task and completed it.

Step 3: What Assessment Tools Can We Use to Measure the Evidence and Provide Specific Criteria to Distinguish Levels of Performance?

The next step was to determine appropriate assessment tools. Again, the teachers had to put on their interdisciplinary assessor hats. What Big Skills

Figure 4.6   An Exploratory Web for "Habitats"

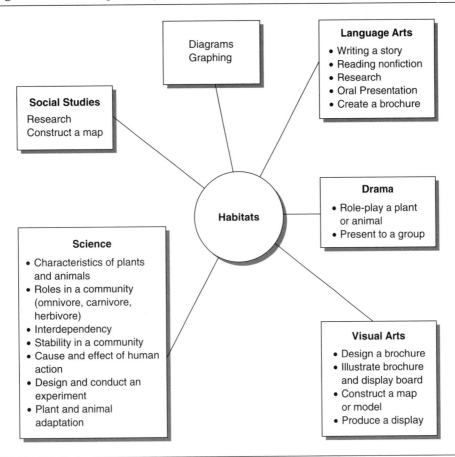

SOURCE: Based on the work of Tom Martin, Phil Teeuwsen, and John Molnar.

and subskills had the students been exposed to as they spiraled through the curriculum? How could the teachers build on this? Were there any new skills that needed to be taught before the students could devise a rubric?

The students had already done some research in other units and had used a research rubric. They knew the subskills involved. The rubric for this Big Skill and its subskills would be reviewed. The criteria to distinguish levels of performance would be discussed. Students could look at exemplars the teacher had collected from previous years as well as assignments that represented lower-quality work. Modifications to the rubric could be made if necessary. This process was similar for the inquiry skills as the students had conducted some experiments already. They had also been exposed to mapping skills and accompanying rubrics, so they could review these and make any necessary modifications.

Although the students had used presentation rubrics before, they needed to learn role-playing skills. This would be a good place for students

Table 4.2   A Big Assessment Task for "Habitats"

Big Assessment Task—"Habitats"

In a group of three, you will decide on a role of a plant or animal in a natural community. Consider choosing an endangered species. In role, you will present your knowledge of your plant/animal and its habitat to the class in a storefront-style display. This presentation must include a visual display on a cardboard structure no larger than two student desks. Be as creative as possible with this display board. The information you need to display is generated from the following activities:

1. Research to identify the distinguishing characteristics of your plant or animal and its habitat. Create a cross-classification chart that includes data on life cycle, needs, food, and enemies. (Research skills)

2. Brainstorm for factors that may affect your plant/animal. Develop a hypothesis and conduct an experiment to test for one or more of these factors. (Hint: This experiment may revolve around testing variables affecting plant growth.) Write a lab report. (Problem-solving skills)

3. Construct a model or map of your habitat indicating significant information. (Design and construction)

4. Produce a brochure on the computer outlining the status of your plant or animal (endangered, threatened, extinct) and the effects of human activity on it. Include what steps can be taken to protect the species and possible future outcomes. (Technological skills)

Your responsibilities include observing and listening to your classmates' presentations and evaluating them using a rubric created by the class. You will also be using the rubric and checklist to evaluate your own presentation. There is teacher evaluation of your research, lab report, brochure, map or model, and your presentation (both for content and role playing).

SOURCE: Tom Martin, Phil Teeuwsen, and John Molnar.

to learn the role-playing skills and to modify the presentation rubric they had already used to reflect the role playing. Finally, they were asked to produce a simple brochure using computer technology. They needed to learn the software and the computer skills to produce such an item. Students would receive a generic product guideline that outlined the criteria for producing an effective brochure, and the teachers would teach the skills that were necessary. Together, they could develop the indicators to distinguish levels of performance.

They developed one rubric for the Big Assessment task that included all the areas that they had considered (Figure 4.7). Concerned with the *be*, these teachers focused on a peer and self-evaluation rubric for teamwork, attitude, and participation. This rubric is offered in Figure 4.8.

Mary Anne McDowell reviewed this unit. She wanted to create a KDB Umbrella with a different emphasis to fit her local context but still cover the mandated curriculum. In her area, the possibility of building a new highway through the local ecosystem was a controversial issue.

Figure 4.7   A Rubric for a Big Assessment Task for "Habitats"

Exploring Plant and Animal Habitats				
	Level 4	**Level 3**	**Level 2**	**Level 1**
Research	Information was very well researched and of appropriate length.	Information was well researched and approximately of appropriate length.	Information was satisfactorily researched and half of the desired length.	Information was not well researched and under half of the desired length.
Visual Presentation	Unique, creative, colorful, and neat	Creative, colorful, and neat	Somewhat creative, colorful, and neat	Lacks creativity, color, and neatness
Oral Presentation	Presenters were knowledgeable about their topic. Audience was interested. Tone of voice, posture, and eye contact were excellent. All areas were covered.	Presenters were knowledgeable about their topic. Audience was interested. Tone of voice, posture, and eye contact were good. Most areas were covered.	Presenters read the research related to their topic. Audience was somewhat interested. Tone of voice, posture, and eye contact were satisfactory; Some ideas covered.	Presenters were unprepared and were not able to offer much information. Audience was disinterested. Tone of voice low. Poor posture. Very little eye contact with audience.
Conventions, Grammar, Spelling, etc.	There are practically no errors or omissions.	There are only a few minor errors and/or omissions.	There are several minor errors and/or omissions.	There are several major and/or consistent errors and/or omissions.

SOURCE: Tom Martin, Phil Teeuwsen, and John Molnar.

Figure 4.8   Peer and Self-Evaluation Rubric for "Habitats"

Peer and Self-Evaluation Rubric				
	Level 4	**Level 3**	**Level 2**	**Level 1**
Teamwork	Helped to decide what the goals of the group were and worked hard to meet these goals.	Accepted and respected the goals of the group and worked hard to meet these goals.	Did not always respect the goals of the group but still worked hard to meet these goals.	Consistently complained about group goals and failed to try as hard as possible to meet the goals.
Attitude	Encouraged others to get involved. Was cooperative and helpful. Expressed opinions in a respectful way. Performed tasks with a positive attitude.	Was cooperative and helpful. Expressed opinions in a respectful way. Performed tasks with a positive attitude.	Was usually cooperative and helpful. Did not always express opinions in a respectful way. Performed tasks with a positive attitude.	Was not very cooperative or helpful. Was not always respectful when expressing opinions. Did not always have a positive attitude.
Participation	Was willing and able to do a number of different tasks within the group.	Was willing and able to do different tasks within the group.	Was willing and able to do a few tasks within the group.	Was not always willing and able to do different tasks within the group.

SOURCE: Tom Martin, Phil Teeuwsen, and John Molnar.

She wanted students to focus on this issue at the same time as they covered the Grade 4 curriculum. Since it was a rich topic, she decided it had to be interdisciplinary. Using the same broad-based science standards as Tom, Phil, and John, but with a different emphasis, she created a similar but different interdisciplinary core assessment task. In her situation, the KDB Umbrella had a different emphasis. For her, it was most important that the students see the impact of humans on the environment and understand that they had a role to play. Figure 4.9 shows Mary Anne's KDB Umbrella.

At this point, Mary Anne could create her Big Assessment task (see Table 4.3). Although her task had many of the same Big Skills and Big

Ideas as the Grade 4 assessment task provided earlier in this chapter, it emphasized a different KDB.

Mary Anne focused on the problem-solving aspect of this situation. She took a real-life situation and embedded the curriculum in it. She had students follow a generic problem-solving model as well as use inquiry skills through a scientific experiment. In developing this assessment task, she kept focus on the KDB Umbrella to make sure she was assessing what she really wanted to assess.

When Mary Anne got to Step 3, she found herself in much the same position as Tom, Phil, and John. Her students were familiar with the Big Skills and had used rubrics to work with the skills before. Now it was a matter of reviewing the rubrics with them and reinforcing the requirements. As for the *be*, she hoped that students would act like environmental stewards, and indeed, in this task, they were inclined to do so. Still, she knew that the ultimate test was not in honoring the environment during this task but in doing so in their daily lives. She could not measure that, but she could instill the importance of that value and the very real conflicts that sometimes accompany such a choice.

In this chapter, we explored interdisciplinary assessment. What is it? How is it done? Who does it, and when? Then we addressed the second question of backward mapping. How do we know when the students have acquired the KDB? Two examples from different grade levels illustrated how the Big Understandings/Ideas and Big Skills spiral through the curriculum. In the next chapter, we will see how to design activities that enable students to demonstrate the KDB.

Figure 4.9   The Know/Do/Be Umbrella for Mary Anne McDowell

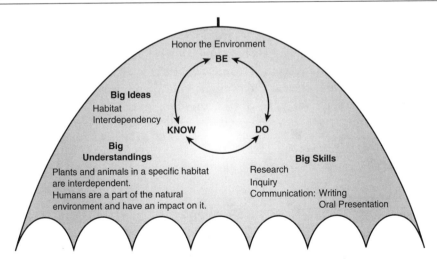

SOURCE: Based on the work of Mary Anne McDowell.

Table 4.3   A Big Assessment Task for Mary Anne McDowell

Big Assessment Task

The city is deciding whether or not to build a highway through the outskirts of town that is still uninhabited. If the highway is built, it will allow people to travel much more quickly from one town to another.

You are the local expert on a (plant/animal). You will give a presentation at the local information session based on your research. Your information will be displayed in a creative way on a cardboard structure no larger than two classroom desks.

Your presentation based on your research must include:

○   The current situation: The characteristics of your _____ and its habitat

○   Introduction of the problem: How will the habitat change with the building of the new highway?

○   What problems are associated with these changes for your _____ ?

○   Generating alternative solutions for solving the problem: A hypothesis and lab report from an experiment and a final recommendation for a solution as it affects your _____

○   A model or map of the current situation and of the recommended solution for the problems caused by the highway.

○   A letter to the city that offers recommendations about how to proceed with the highway emphasizing problems and solutions for your _____ habitat.

○   You will read this letter at the forum for highway planning and will be willing to enter general discussions.

Your responsibilities include observing and listening to your classmates' presentations and evaluating them using a rubric created by the class. You will also use the rubric and checklist to evaluate your own presentation. There will be teacher evaluation of all parts of your presentation.

SOURCE: Mary Anne McDowell.

DISCUSSION QUESTIONS

1. Consider some of the assessments that you have experienced as a student or teacher. Were there any interdisciplinary aspects to these assessments? If not, could there have been?

2. What benefits can you see from assessing more than one subject at a time?

3. What problems can you envision when assessing more than one subject at a time? Are there any clear ways to solve these problems?

4. Differentiate between assessment tasks and assessment tools. When can these be considered interdisciplinary?

5. Who do you believe is responsible for teaching cross-disciplinary skills? Why? How might this happen in your own context?

6. Review the three steps to creating a Big Assessment task. The first step has three parts:
   Step 1 What is the KDB? What are the generic criteria that demonstrate the KDB?
   Step 2 What broad-based standards in the curriculum documents can represent the KDB?
   Step 3 What are the possible activities and assessments embedded in the standards?

   Step 2 is to decide what assessment tasks could act as evidence to show the KDB. Step 3 is to select assessment tools to provide specific criteria and measure the levels of performance. This sounds like a very complex process, but it is easier when you actually do it. Can you describe this process in your own words? Why are all the parts necessary?

7. Compare the path of Tom, Phil, and John to Mary Anne's path. They have both used the same set of standards. How are they the same, yet different? Why did the author include such similar examples?

8. "The key to a relevant curriculum is a relevant and challenging Big Assessment task." Do you believe this? What does this statement mean to you?

SUGGESTED ACTIVITIES

In each of the following chapters, you will find activities that build on each other. It is best if you choose a specific grade level to work at continue to build on your work in the activities for each chapter.

1. Analyze the Toward Nanotechnology Big Assessment task. What makes this a good assessment task? The assessment tool measures language skills because the teachers already had a lot of data on science. How could they have made this task interdisciplinary?

2. Do a preliminary Scan and Cluster to identify a set of broad-based standards from more than one subject area. (You might want to begin with the Scan and Cluster in Chapter 3). Create an exploratory web (Figure 4.4) to see possible activities embedded in the standards. Create the KDB Umbrella.

3. Once the KDB Umbrella is created, you have enough information to create a Big Assessment task. After you have selected the task, write an assessment task statement in a way that you would present it to students. Be sure to follow the criteria for a well-written assessment task.

4. Select good assessment tools to measure success. Do these tools really measure what you want to measure? Why? Do they connect back to the KDB Umbrella?

5

How Do I Create Learning Experiences That Lead to the Know/Do/Be?

In this chapter, we explore how to create integrated learning experiences that enable students to attain the required standards. This means that the learning experiences must be connected both to the Big Assessment task and to the Know/Do/Be (KDB). An effective strategy to connect daily learning experiences to the Big Picture is to work with Big Questions. In this chapter, we explore how to create Big Questions and how to differentiate these from unit questions. Finally, we look at the task of internal alignment of the day-by-day instructional activities with appropriate assessment tools and standards.

CREATING BIG QUESTIONS TO ALIGN THE KDB AND BIG ASSESSMENT TASKS

Big Questions and Unit Questions

Big Questions align the KDB and the Big Assessment task. They also act as a focus for planning the unit. In addition, there are usually unit questions that zoom in on the specific content to be covered. Big Questions are different from unit questions. Unit questions are subject specific. They are written in "kid speak," pose a problem or reveal a controversy, or ask students to prove a point. Unit questions help the students answer the Big Question and address the Big Understanding. In Figure 5.1, Schmied (2005) offers examples of Big Questions and unit questions.

Big Questions cut across the disciplines and relate to the real world. Because they are open-ended, they require an interdisciplinary approach to answer them. They lead to other questions and are engaging to students. As in Big Understandings, Big Questions are timeless, cross-cultural, universal, and written at the conceptual level.

Big Questions are meaty questions that require higher-order thinking. Some experts suggest that to ensure higher-order thinking, it is best to begin an essential question with a "why" or "how" rather than a "what," "when," or "where."

- How does a community work together effectively?
- How do cultures affect one another?
- How can you measure freedom?
- Why do different cultures use land differently?

Figure 5.1   Big Questions and Unit Questions

Big Questions	Unit Questions
How does culture define conflict?	What is conflict? How did culture influence the way Americans reacted to English laws in 1776? How do differing cultures express conflict?
How are patterns seen in systems?	What is a variable? What is a system of equations? How do you solve a system of linear equations with two variables?
How do values influence decision making?	What is the role of values in your life? How does Tom Sawyer's decision show/demonstrate what he thinks is important? How are decisions related to core values?

- How do religious conflicts from the past affect us today?
- Why is *x* heroic?

Wiggins and McTighe (2005) argue that Big Questions do not have to begin with "why" or "how." Instead, they can begin with any adverb as long as they are wide-open questions that lead to a rich inquiry:

- What is love?
- What is the purpose of life?
- Who is the master of the universe?
- Where is your real home?

Creating Big Questions From Across the Curriculum

I attended a workshop in which Kathy Schmied (www.plsweb.com) introduced me to an intriguing process to create Big Questions. Participants in her workshop formed groups of four. Each group was given playdough and a card that said either "A bird has a beak" or "Life forms are equipped with the tools needed to survive." We were asked to keep what was on our card a secret from the other groups and to make a representation with the playdough of the statement on our card. No one realized that Kathy had given out equal numbers of only these two statements.

Kathy asked us to share our representations and asked these questions:

- Why did you choose this item to represent your creation?
- Did you have an image in your mind prior to your creation?
- What type of discussion did your group have prior to creating your representation?
- How were the different creations connected to the statements given to the groups?
- How do the statements differ?
- How did the differences in the statements affect the outcomes?

It was fascinating to see the different creations that were produced. Each group that had received the bird statement created a representation that was clearly a bird with a beak. The groups that had received the statement "Life forms are equipped with the tools needed to survive" created a wide variety of representations for the statement. Kathy pointed out that the bird statement was a "fact" and that the life forms statement was a "conceptual statement."

Kathy emphasized that the difference between a fact statement and a conceptual statement meant a difference not only in the end product but also in the approach and planning for the representation. Those of us who received the conceptual statement spent time in rich discussion about what the statement meant and how to best represent it. In contrast, the participants with the factual card did not have to spend time deciding what a bird was. Kathy noted that this is true in teaching situations as well. When we work at the factual level, we do not need to challenge our thinking. When we work at the conceptual level, we need to engage in higher-order thinking.

My experience in the workshop illustrated to me how difficult it may be for some teachers to accept the ambiguity around forming Big Questions. When my group received the "Life forms are equipped with the tools needed to survive" statement, one person in the group offered her answer. When each of the other three group members offered a different interpretation, the first person angrily argued that hers was the "right answer" and that we should create our representation based on it. While the rest of us entered a rich discussion about the various things the statement could mean, the first person physically withdrew from the group.

A Formula for Big Questions

Schmied offers a simple, but effective, formula for writing Big Questions:

Concept + Verb + Concept

This could be interpreted as:

Big Idea + Verb + Big Idea

She had us develop a work bank that was filled with verbs that work well in creating Big Questions. Here are some examples of good verbs:

- Guide
- Relate
- Promote
- Influence
- Provoke
- Change
- Affect
- Perpetuate
- Diminish
- Help
- Transform

To create good questions, teachers connect interdisciplinary Big Ideas with a verb to create a question that begins with "how" or "why." The following questions are further examples:

- How do resources promote conflict?
- How do social inequities provoke civil war?
- Why does culture perpetuate conflict?
- How do values influence decision making?

Connecting Big Questions to Big Understandings

Using Schmied's system, teachers will create their own Big Questions and thus will potentially create Big Understandings. Alternatively, they can use this same process to create Big Understandings and then move to Big Questions (Figure 5.2). Once more, the curriculum designer must recognize that this will not be a linear process; the designer may return more than once to places he or she has passed before.

Developing Big Questions From Big Understandings

Sometimes the Big Questions are developed from the standards themselves. Usually such a question involves a broad-based standard found in

Figure 5.2   Creating Big Understandings and Big Questions

Big Understandings	←→	Big Questions
Cultures define conflict.	←→	How does culture define conflict?
Patterns occur in all systems.	←→	How are patterns seen in systems?
Individual values influence decision making.	←→	How do values influence decision making?
The use, distribution, and significance of resources are affected by the interaction of humans with physical resources.	←→	How are the use, distribution, and significance of resources affected by the interaction of humans with physical resources?
Art reflects and shapes culture.	←→	Why does art reflect and shape culture?
Patterns are often revealed through statistical analysis, and how do they enable prediction.	←→	What patterns are often revealed through statistical analysis, and they enable prediction?
Diet affects health, appearance, and performance.	←→	Why does diet affect health, appearance, and performance?

one discipline, often from a science or social studies document. However, the Big Understanding can involve other subject areas. This was illustrated in Figure 5.2.

You met Tom Martin, Phil Teeuwsen, and John Molnar, as well as Mary Anne McDowell, in the last chapter. They developed their Big Questions from the overall expectations in the Grade 4 science curriculum guidelines for a unit on life systems (www.edu.gov.on.ca). These broad-based standards also acted as their Big Understandings. Figure 5.3 illustrates this connection.

Mary Anne McDowell used the same broad-based science standards as her Grade 4 colleagues, but as we explored in Chapter 4, her emphasis was different than theirs. She wanted her Big Questions to reflect the Big Understandings she had created from the broad-based standards (Figure 5.4).

Figure 5.3   Creating Big Understandings and Big Questions From Broad-Based Standards

Broad-Based, Standards		Big Understandings		Big Questions Topic Questions
Demonstrate an understanding of the concepts of habitat and community and identify the factors that could affect habitats and communities of plants and animals.		→		What factors affect plant and animal habitats and communities?
Investigate the dependency of plants and animals on their habitat and the interrelationships of the plants and the animals living in a specific habitat.	→	All living things are conncected.	→	How do plants and animals interact with their habitat and with each other?
Describe ways in which humans can change habitats and the effects of these changes on the plants and animals within the habitat.	→	Humans are a part of the natural environment. Living things adapt to their environment.	→	What are the effects of humans on plant and animal communities?

SOURCE: Tom Martin, Phil Teeuwsen, and John Molnar.

Figure 5.4   Mary Anne McDowell's Big Understandings and Big Questions From Broad-Based Standards

Broad-Based, Standards →	Big Understandings →	Big Questions Topic Questions
Investigate the dependency of plants and animals on their habitat and the interrelationships of the plants and the animals living in a specific habitat. →	Plants and animals in a specific habitat are interdependent. →	How are plants and animals in a specific environment interdependent?
Describe ways in which humans can change habitats and the effects of these changes on the plants and animals within the habitat. →	Humans are a part of the natural environment. and have an impact on it. →	How are humans a part of the natural environment, and what impact to they have on it? What potential impact do humans have on their environment for better or worse?

SOURCE: Mary Anne McDowell.

A PERSONAL INSIGHT IN DESIGNING INSTRUCTIONAL STRATEGIES

As I began to write this chapter, I was asked to take on a course in educational administration for a Chinese cohort of master's of education students. These students had just arrived in Canada and had little experience in the North American approach to teaching. Educational administration is not my area of expertise, but the original instructor had fallen ill and the university desperately needed someone to step in. Since I had worked with a Chinese cohort before and had a passing knowledge of educational administration, I was elected. Although I did not have a list of standards to cover, I had a compulsory textbook to follow. When I skimmed the textbook, I was appalled. It was absolutely deadly. I could hardly bear to read it myself. The vocabulary was so difficult that an English speaker would have trouble. How would a Chinese student new to North America fare?

I was in despair. Then I realized I could apply exactly the same principles that I was writing about in this chapter. I did not need to be limited by a presentation of a deadly textbook. I could cover the material and still make it interesting. The textbook could be the backdrop for the *know* of the course. From it, I could pull the Big Ideas and Big Understandings. Then I could use the text selectively to teach these. This would leave room for alternate readings. I believed that the students needed to learn and demonstrate graduate skills such as research, critical thinking, and academic writing (*do*). But I also thought they should learn leadership skills, such as how to give a good oral presentation. Finally, I wanted them to be active independent learners (*be*), a concept that was new for most students.

I personally was concerned about how these students could return to China as educational leaders if they had no vision of education. For me, that vision involved a constructivist approach to teaching and learning. I wanted them to know about constructivism, yet the textbook allotted only 13 of 442 pages to constructivist teaching. Also, none of their other courses would focus on this as subject matter. There was so much information that I wanted to cover, it was difficult to see any other method of teaching other than a three-hour lecture each week.

While writing this chapter, I suddenly saw the light. I could teach the content with a constructivist approach. Students would actually experience this type of pedagogy. They would learn it by doing it. The content would be educational administration as described in the text. But the students would also gain knowledge of constructivism by hands-on learning. Using the textbook with this perspective, I developed a KDB Umbrella (Figure 5.5).

Figure 5.5   The Know/Do/Be Umbrella for the Chinese Cohort

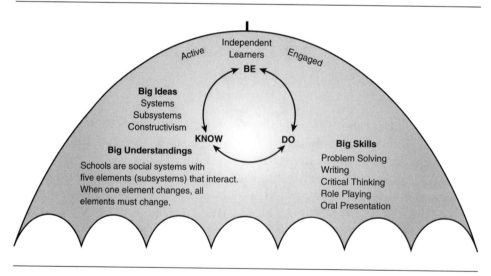

Creating a Big Assessment Task

Once I had established the KDB Umbrella, I could develop the Big Assessment task. It was as follows:

> You are invited to a forum on the Future of Education in China as one of two experts in (one element in the school system, for example, experts in organizational development, leadership, school culture, or psychology). Please collaborate with the other expert to decide on what you will say and how you will share this role as expert. In role, you will present your vision of an ideal, but realistic, future for education in China. As well, you will need to have some ideas on how your vision could be implemented.
>
> The chair of this forum will ask further questions based on issues you studied in the courses you took this semester. This will be an open forum, and you may speak freely and out of role. Your task here is to be convincing. You will be more convincing if you strengthen your opinion with data (theory).

Now I needed to create the weekly activities. I matched the chapters in the book (my standards) with the KDB. I was delighted by how well this worked. I was constantly able to refer back to the KDB as we plowed through the text. It helped make sense of the Big Picture for the Chinese cohort, a Big Picture that was unfamiliar to them. Also, I was able to connect to their own experiences, which were vastly different in most cases from the North American experiences.

For the culminating activity, students spoke at the forum at the university to a small audience interested in the future of China. It was clear that they had a good knowledge base in their area of expertise. Also, they were able to discuss the future of education in general terms that included a constructivist approach. They also made vast improvements in English and had acquired good presentation skills.

A more telling marker of the success of this approach was reflected in their exit portfolios. Students prepared portfolios in which they synthesized the most important things they had learned in the program. I was delighted and surprised when almost all of them used the work that they had done in this class as the foundation for this synthesis and chose "systems thinking" as a way to integrate their learning across all their courses.

TWO PRINCIPLES FOR DESIGNING DAILY ACTIVITIES AND ASSESSMENTS

How do we design the daily activities? Once the KDB Umbrella is created, the Big Assessment task articulated, and the Big Questions developed, it is time to set up the daily activities and assessments. Only after having done this preliminary work can the daily activities be aligned effectively with the rest of the curriculum. Yet there is more to the curriculum than alignment to consider. Once again, we need to think about both accountability and relevance. The following strategies help ensure that the curriculum delivers both.

Principle 1: Using Two-Dimensional Thinking

Curriculum designers must use their two-dimensional thinking to create the day-to-day activities. The daily activities must be aligned with the Big Picture (the KDB and the Big Assessment tasks). At the same time, each activity must address a standard and have an accompanying assessment strategy. Thus, the instructional activities are aligned in two dimensions. There needs to be a constant double-check that any planned daily activity or assessment indeed leads to the Big Assessment task and the KDB. Figure 5.6 shows how one works in two dimensions.

Principle 2: Learning Principles as an Assessment Guide

Perhaps the most essential ingredient to guide any curriculum planning is how people learn best. We know a lot about how people learn through research on the brain, learning styles, and multiple intelligences. By tapping into our own experiences and applying research findings, we can construct a list of learning principles.

Figure 5.6   Using Two-Dimensional Thinking to Create Daily Activities

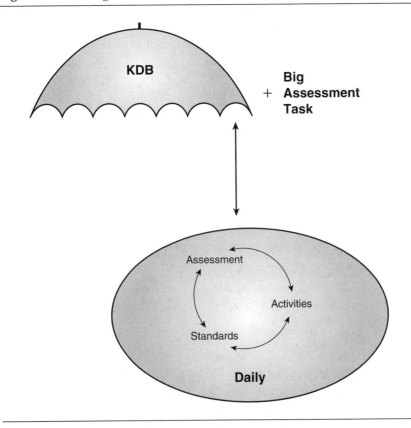

Using these principles as a primary guide for our lesson planning, we can also think about activities and assessment in a new way. Instructional activities should follow these principles if we wish optimum learning to occur. Assessment should also follow the learning principles. Assessment, in fact, can and should enhance learning. Using a backward design approach, we can also think of instructional activities as assessment tasks. Every activity has an embedded assessment. The assessment may be as simple as teacher observation or as complex as creating a portfolio. Figure 5.7 shows how learning principles can be linked to assessment and teaching.

But how do teachers make the instruction relevant and motivating when there is so much to think about? I would suggest rethinking the traditional starting point of planning engaging activities that students enjoy. If a teacher begins with interesting but challenging assessment tasks, then the daily activities will also be interesting and challenging. Assessment and instruction become almost interchangeable. The assessment is embedded in the instructional task, and the instructional tasks are embedded in the assessment. This means that every instructional activity will have an assessment component—whether it is assessment "of," "for," or "as" learning.

CONNECTING TO THE KDB IN DAILY ACTIVITIES AND ASSESSMENTS

The same Big Understandings/Ideas and Big Skills spiral throughout the curriculum from K to 12. This spiraling can only really be seen when a vertical scan is done. Thus, as students progress through the grades, they will deepen their understanding of the most important things to know, do, and be. Their tasks will be more sophisticated and complex. And presumably when they enter the real world as adults, they will be aware of the major problems of today and have a head start on handling them. How do teachers connect to the KDB on a daily basis? We will explore this question for the *know, do,* and *be.*

The *Know*

Although most curriculum documents stress the teaching of concepts, this is a murky area for some teachers. How does one teach concept attainment? Figure 5.8 offers levels of understanding for interdisciplinary Big Understandings. In this chart, the Big Understandings increase in complexity and unfamiliarity for the learner. The levels could easily be adapted for a rubric. Figure 5.9 offers levels of understanding for growth in concept attainment—the Big Ideas. The levels begin with an understanding of a Big Idea in a discipline first and move to a more interdisciplinary understanding. Again, these levels could easily be adapted to a rubric.

Figure 5.7   Alignment of Learning Principles With Instructional Activities and Embedded Assessments

Learning Principles	Instructional Strategies	Embedded Assessments
Learn by doing	Active learning	Assess the doing Performance assessment
Material is relevant	Activities are personally relevant	Meaningful assessment that students can learn from
Making connections	Connects to real-life, personal experiences, across disciplines	Embedded assessment
Fun, enjoyable	Enjoyable, fun	Enjoyable element
Challenging	High standards	Assessment embodies high standards
Clear expectations	Teacher is explicit about criteria for success	Assessment matches these criteria
Ongoing feedback	Includes ongoing feedback	Assessment is ongoing
Learn in different ways at different rates	Choices. Allow for different ways to reach standards to allow for different learning styles and Multiple Intelligences.	Choice of assessments related to different activities
Reflection	Build in time for reflection	Journals, discussion, quiet time, self-assessment, peer assessment
Metacognition	Metacognition strategies	Assess metacognition
Positive reinforcement	Variety of positive reinforcements built into activity. Supportive environment.	Ongoing assessment includes constructive criticism and opportunity to redo.
Variety	Use variety in teaching strategies	Use variety in assessment strategies
Learn by teaching	Teach others-jigsaw puzzle, tutoring, demonstration	Self-assessment, peer assessment
Modeling	Teacher walks the talk	Teacher self-assessment, student assessment of teacher

The *Do*

Students are required to demonstrate the Big Skills from K to 12 and indeed throughout life as an adult. These skills are interdisciplinary. They

Figure 5.8   Levels of Understanding for Attaining the Big Understandings

	Beginning	Developing	Competent	Proficient	Expert
Level of Understanding	The learner can identify and explain a Big Understanding or relationship within a topic.	The learner can provide novel examples of the Big Understandings across events, topics, and fields of studies or disciplines.	The learner can use knowledge about Big Understandings in various disciplines or topics to develop an inter-disciplinary theme or generalization.	The learner searches for inter-disciplinary themes or generalizations in unfamiliar information in order to identify analogous or equivalent situations.	The learner searches for inter-disciplinary themes or Big Understandings in unfamiliar information in order to identify analogous or equivalent situations and develop solutions to real-life problems.

SOURCE: Figure 4.16 from Carol Tomlinson, Sandra Kaplan, Joseph Renzulli, Jeanne Purcell, Jann Leppien, and Deborah Burns. (2002). *The Parallel Curriculum* (p. 146). Reprinted by permission of the publisher, Corwin Press, 2002.

may vary slightly in each discipline, but the core of the skill remains the same. Thus, it is crucial for students to know the criteria for the Big Skills and to learn specifically how to demonstrate these criteria.

Generic assessment tools are a good way to get a picture of the Big Skills. Generic rubrics are particularly helpful. The catch is to ensure that a rubric measures what it is intended to measure. Many rubrics are available now through textbooks, educational resources, and the Internet. There are holistic and analytic trait rubrics. A holistic rubric combines the important ingredients of a performance or product to allow an overall impression of the student's work. Such a rubric is helpful for a simple task or to allow for a snapshot of overall quality. The analytical trait rubric analyzes a product or performance so that each criterion can be addressed separately. There is detailed feedback. The analytical rubric helps students to zero in on the subskills they must acquire to demonstrate the Big Skill.

Also, there are generic rubrics and task-specific rubrics. The generic rubric can be used for similar performances across a variety of situations. The same general rubric can be used for all open-ended mathematical

Figure 5.9   Levels of Understanding for Attaining the Big Ideas

	Beginning	Developing	Competent	Proficient	Expert
Level of Understanding	The learner can define and provide key attributes that distinguish disciplinary Big Ideas in a given field or discipline.	The learner can use the concept to categorize and understand new information in the same field or discipline.	The learner can identify commonalities between disciplinary Big Ideas in one field or topic and disciplinary Big Ideas in another field or discipline.	The learner can classify and name comparable disciplinary Big Ideas in two or more fields as interdisciplinary Big Ideas.	When confronted with new information in another discipline, students attempt to classify the information using an interdisciplinary Big Idea
Example	Migration is the purposeful movement of living things across regions.	Migration is evident during the 1880s and early 1930s and the 1940s in various parts of the United States.	The migration of whales has several things in common with the migration of human beings.	The concept of beneficial movement is evident in both biology and anthropology.	The population in our small rural town experienced a decline in the 2006 census. I wonder if migration is a factor.

SOURCE: Figure 5.7 from Carol Tomlinson, Sandra Kaplan, Joseph Renzulli, Jeanne Purcell, Jann Leppien, and Deborah Burns. (2002). *The Parallel Curriculum* (p. 145). Reprinted by permission of the publisher, Corwin Press, 2002.

thinking, for all oral presentations, or for all interpersonal skills. The task-specific rubric is designed for only one task. Armed with a battery of generic rubrics, the teacher can create task-specific ones without reinventing the wheel each time. Taking this approach allows both the teacher and the student to see the Big Picture. Figure 5.10 shows a generic rubric for an oral presentation.

The *Be*

Although *being* is frequently not addressed, I believe it should be. If we don't assess something, then it is not perceived as valuable. There are many ways that the *be* can be addressed. Students can self-monitor their

Figure 5.10   A Generic Rubric for Oral Presentation

	Poor	Adequate	Average	Good	Excellent
Good introduction	1	2	3	4	5
Evidence of research and preparation Material explained thoroughly	1	2	3	4	5
Eye contact Tone of voice Confident	1	2	3	4	5
Aware of audience understanding, and adjusted presentation	1	2	3	4	5
Addressed questions well	1	2	3	4	5
Use of audiovisuals or multimedia	1	2	3	4	5
Overall impact Interesting presentation that gave a fresh perspective	1	2	3	4	5
Total					
Comments:					

work and do a self-assessment. This type of self-monitoring is really about a student's work ethic. Interpersonal skills are often measured through teamwork. A growth portfolio has the value of "growth" embedded into it. This growth is not always about content and skills but revolves around personal growth. Journals can veer into the *be* territory and can be evaluated for personal insights.

Figure 5.11 offers a rubric for the *be* developed by Tom Martin, John Molnar, and Phillip Teeuwsen. It is a generic rubric that can be used at any grade level and in any context. They used this rubric in the example offered in Chapter 4.

Big Assessment Task

The Big Assessment task will involve all three aspects of the KDB. Figure 5.12 offers a generic rubric for a typical culminating activity. Students are required to create an exhibit that includes an oral presentation, an interactive activity, and a display of the research. These tasks will require an interaction of the *know* and *do*. Students are expected to *be* good team members. This is reflected in the Interpersonal category. Students are assessed individually on this aspect. Bernice Stieva, Po-Ling Bork, Gail Higenell, and Hsiang-Yi (Alice) Kuo created this rubric for a Grade 6 unit on birds of prey. It could be adapted easily to similar culminating activities, and it quickly allows the students to see what they need to *know, do,* and *be* for this unit. Each subset of this rubric could be developed into a more detailed rubric depending on the situation.

HOW LYDIA JANIS DEVELOPED THE DAILY ACTIVITIES AND ASSESSMENTS

In this section, we will follow my interpretation of Lydia Janis's curriculum development on the Civil War for the fifth grade. Lydia was a teacher whose teaching practice was described in a book called *The Parallel Curriculum* (Tomlinson et al., 2002). Lydia followed the principles advocated in this book. She integrated history, government, geography, and economics. The learning principles were always at the forefront of the thinking.

Lydia's first challenge was whether to follow the objectives from her textbook or the state standards. As she read the state standards, she found that they did capture key understandings that students needed in order to understand this period in history but also allowed her to develop more enduring Big Ideas/Understandings and Big Skills. The broad-based standard that guided her curriculum design was the following: "Demonstrate an in-depth understanding of major events and trends in U.S. history."

The Civil War provided the specific content for doing this. She could use parts of her text for the content. Also, many of the state standards in

Figure 5.11   A Generic Rubric for the *Be*

		LEARNING SKILLS CHECKLIST (BE)		
	Excellent	**Good**	**Satisfactory**	**Needs Improvement**
Responsible	Assumes leadership responsibilities in groups Demonstrates leadership and works effectively with others	Assumes responsibilities in groups Willingly works with others	Assumes simple responsibilities in small groups Works with a limited number of peers	Avoids responsibilities, even in small groups Reluctant to work with others
Cooperative	Establishes positive relationships with peers and adults Works effectively without supervision	Establishes positive relationships with peers and adults Works well without supervision	Usually establishes positive relationships with peers and adults Works well with supervision	Reluctant to establish positive relationships with peers Requires direct supervision
Independent	Follows routines and instructions independently Generates many questions for further inquiry	Follows routines and instructions independently Generates questions for further inquiry	Follows routines and instructions with some assistance Sometimes generates questions for further inquiry	Rarely follows routines and instructions without support Generates questions for further inquiry reluctantly and only with assistance
Inquisitive	Shows keen interest and curiosity about a wide variety of objects and events	Shows interest and curiosity about objects and events	Shows some interest and curiosity about objects and events	Shows interest and curiosity about a very limited number of objects and events
Creative	Develops many original ideas and creative solutions to solve problems Applies a variety of successful strategies to new problem situations	Develops original ideas and creative solutions to solve problems Applies successful strategies to new problem situations	Develops ideas and solutions to solve problems with some assistance Applies some strategies to new problem situations	Develops ideas and solutions to solve problems only with assistance Applies a limited number of strategies to new problem situations

SOURCE: Tom Martin, Phil Teeuwsen, and John Molnar.

Figure 5.12 A Sample of a Big Assessment Task Rubric

LEARNING SKILLS CHECKLIST (BE)

	Excellent	Good	Satisfactory	Needs Improvement	Unsatisfactory
Content	All elements are present, neatly and correctly labelled. Each element has a function and clearly serves to illustrate some aspect of the project.	Most elements are present, neatly and correctly labelled. Each element has a function and clearly serves to illustrate some aspect of the project.	Most elements are present, neatly and correctly labelled. Some elements have a function and serve to illustrate some aspect of the project.	Elements are incomplete and chaotic, without a clear plan.	Most elements are missing. Overall display is chaotic.
Diagrams Charts Sketches Graphs	Diagrams, charts, and/or sketches are clear and greatly add to understanding.	Diagrams, charts, and/or sketches are clear and easy to understand.	Diagrams, charts, and/or sketches are somewhat difficult to understand.	Diagrams, charts, and/or sketches are difficult to understand or not appropriate.	Diagrams, charts, and/or sketches are missing.
Display	Display is attractive, easy to read, neat, and securely attached. Extra details are present.	Display is attractive, well organized, easy to read, neat, and securely attached.	Display is somewhat organized, easy to read, neat, and securely attached.	Display is not organized or is somewhat unclear.	Display is unorganized, difficult to read, and sloppy.
Presentation	Each student in the group can clearly explain.	Each student in the group can explain most of the information.	Eact student in the group can explain with prompting.	One of the students in the group cannot explain.	All students have difficulty explaining.
Individual Interpersonal Skills	Student almost always listens to, shares with, and supports efforts of others in the group.	Student usually listens to, shares with, and supports efforts of others in the group	Student sometimes listens to and shares with others in the group.	Student rarely listens to or shares with others in the group.	Student works on their own with no regard for others.

SOURCE: Bernice Stieva, Po-Ling Bork, Gail Higenell, and Hsiang-Yi (Alice) Kuo.

social studies could fall under this broad-based standard and allow for the creation of a relevant curriculum.

Lydia developed her own set of the KDB as follows:

Know:

Big Understanding

All conflicts have causes.

The key to resolving conflicts is a comprehensive understanding of related causes and effects.

Big Ideas

Cause and effect

Conflict resolution

Do:

Develop an argument, research

Be:

Able to resolve conflict

At this point, Lydia could develop her Big Assessment task. It was as follows:

Table 5.1   A Big Assessment Task for the Civil War

Big Assessment Task
You wil create a Civil War quilt that demonstrates the important Big Understands and Big Ideas of the time. You will work individually, or in groups of two, three, or four. Develop a visual plan for the Civil War Quilt. Your quilt must depict the following: ❑ Key people and events of the Civil War period ❑ Cultures, economies and livelihoods of various groups in the North and South ❑ The roots and consequences of slavery ❑ Varied viewpoints and perspectives and the resulting conflicts ❑ How conflict resolution and compromise mediated these conflicts ❑ Other important conclusions about this period. Individually, you will write a reflective piece to interpret your quilt, and how it demonstrate the six requirements. Support your conclusions with

Daily Activities and Assessments

Lydia began her unit with a pre- and postassessment that focused on the conceptual learning of the unit. She provided an initial word bank of Big Ideas revolving around the Civil War. Students created a concept map using the word bank and provided concrete examples of the Big Ideas. In the concept map, the students drew lines to connecting Big Ideas and Big Understandings. To measure student growth in concept attainment during the unit, she used the rubric in Figure 5.13.

She also used a generic checklist to teach the Big Skill for developing a strong argument. This checklist is in Figure 5.14.

Now Lydia could fully prepare her daily lessons. For an introductory activity, Lydia prepared a flowchart to show the major concepts of the Civil War in history, economics, geography, and government. She used open-ended discussion questions to generate student interest and to facilitate making connections with previous experiences and student interests. She used Civil War photographs that depicted a pattern and a relationship. She used these photos to demonstrate the kind of analysis she wanted students to make.

During the unit, Lydia used teaching methods that were inductive. All activities and assessments were related to the Big Assessment task and her KDB Umbrella. Students were given a wide range of materials such as data; tables; graphs; photographs; journals of women, slaves, and soldiers; and actual newspaper articles. She asked open-ended questions and used Socratic Big Ideas questioning. During the activities, students constantly searched for such as patterns, relationships, causes and effects. She used large- and small-group strategies to support student analysis and concept attainment through discussion, shared inquiry, think-pair-share activities, and debriefings. Ongoing assessment was provided through the products created during daily activities such as document analysis, reflective journals, and concept maps.

Lydia also had students role-play a re-creation of the Lincoln/Douglas debate and the *Dred Scott* decision. Her students examined varying perspectives on the rights of people versus the rights of the state, and they had to prove their points of view with legitimate evidence. Small-group reflections followed as well as a large-group debriefing. Here, students articulated the Big Ideas and Big Understandings.

At the same time, Lydia modified activities to account for different learning styles. For students with learning difficulties, she provided different print documents to support analytical reading. She worked with students needing individual help and held conferences with some to scaffold their concept-based learning. Students with writing difficulties could tape-record their reflective analysis for the Big Assessment task. For the more advanced students, she provided more challenging questions and more sophisticated print documents. At all times, Lydia was conscious of aligning the standards, activities, and assessments.

Figure 5.13 Lydia's Rubric for Concept Development

	Beginning	Developing	Competent	Proficient	Expert
Level of Understanding	The learner Can Communicate the term associated with an abstract concept.	The learner Can Paraphrase the definition of a concept.	The learner can provide examples and non-examples of the concept.	The learner can provide key attributes that distinguish the concept category.	The learner can link the concept with other related concepts.
Example	"Civil"	"*Civil* means something to do with citizens of a place. A civil war is a war fought inside a Country and among its citizens".	Examples: "I am a citizen of the United States." "I am not a citizen of Russia." "World war II Was not a civil war." "The recent war in Ireland was a civil war."	Citizens Members State Nation Law Rights Public	"People have civil wars when they can't resolve their conflicts or achieve their rights peacefully.

SOURCE: Figure 4.16 from Carol Tomlinson, Sandra Kaplan, Joseph Renzulli, Jeanne Purcell, Jann Leppien, and Deborah Burns. (2002). *The Parallel Curriculum* (p. 117). Reprinted by permission of the publisher, Corwin Press, 2002.

TEACHER THINKING AND THE RED HILL UNIT

Let's look at the thinking behind Vladia Jusko McBrain, Rumeeza Salim, and Susan McLachlin Grade 7 unit called the Red Hill unit. They integrated science, geography, and English. Interestingly, this unit is quite similar to both the one developed by John, Phil, and Tom and the one developed by Mary Anne for Grade 4 (Chapter 4). They all developed units for strands under the rubric of life systems in science. For Grade 4, the topic was "habitats and communities." For Grade 7, it was "interactions within the ecosystem." Clearly, these units will build on the same Big Understandings and Big Ideas. In Mary Anne's and the Red Hill case, the students used an immediate and significant environmental issue in their area. For the Red Hill unit, the proposed highway would cut through a

Figure 5.14 Checklist: Developing a Strong Argument

Developing a Strong Argument

❑ Clearly states the claim or argument

❑ Provides sufficient evidence related to the claim or argument

❑ Selects credible evidence sources

❑ Consults multiple sources

❑ Selects relevant evidence

❑ Clearly explains all assumptions

❑ Provides a logical argument

❑ Refutes alternative claims or arguments

SOURCE: Figure 4.18 from Carol Tomlinson, Sandra Kaplan, Joseph Renzulli, Jeanne Purcell, Jann Leppien, and Deborah Burns. (2002). *The Parallel Curriculum* (p. 118). Reprinted by permission of the publisher, Corwin Press.

sensitive environmental area and a culturally significant site and would arguably violate aboriginal rights.

Step 1

Vladia, Rumeeza, and Susan started with a Scan and Cluster of the science, English, and social sciences documents (www.edu.gov.on.ca). They found a natural fit for geography (themes of geography) and science (life systems: interactions within ecosystems). They selected four broad-based factors to guide their work.

Geography standard:

- Produce a report on current environmental events in the news.
- Use the five themes of geography (location/place, environment, region, interaction, and movement) to focus your inquiry.

Science standard:

- Investigate the interactions in an ecosystem, and identify factors that affect the balance among components of an ecosystem.
- Demonstrate an understanding of the effects of human activities and technological innovations as well as the effects of changes that take place naturally on the sustainability of ecosystems.

A broad-based *English standard* would also guide the planning:

- Produce pieces of writing using a variety of forms, techniques, and resources appropriate to the form and purpose.

Now they were ready to create the KDB Umbrella. It is seen in Figure 5.15. Once the Grade 7 team had created the KDB Umbrella, they reviewed the standards for suggestions about the kind of activities that should be included in the unit. This helped them to move on to the second step.

Figure 5.15   The Know/Do/Be Umbrella for Red Hill

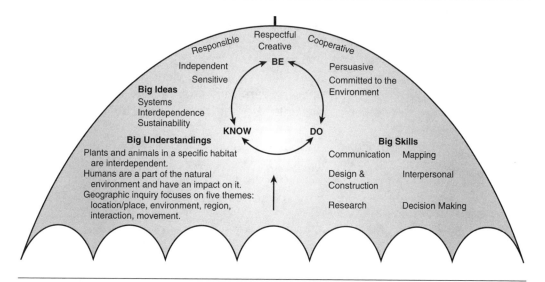

SOURCE: Based on the work of Vladia Jusko McBrian, Rumeeza Salim, and Susan McLachlin.

Step 2

To create the Big Assessment task, Vladia, Rumeeza, and Susan needed to continually check that the task aligned to the KDB Umbrella. Indeed, the task needed to provide evidence that the students had achieved the KDB. An adapted version of their task follows:

> You have been invited to present at an environmental forum. Research a specific environmental issue. Locate that area on a map. In groups of three, prepare a seminar presentation on this issue. One person should represent the viewpoint of an environmentalist. One should be a representative who opposes environmental protection (perhaps a representative of big business who is lobbying for the change to the natural environment). The third person plays a government official

(Continued)

(Continued)

> who is looking for a compromise that will satisfy both groups. Present the three sides to the audience. Use data to support your opinions. Be sure to think about the five themes of geography in your analysis. Bring in visuals such as maps, graphs, notes, reports, and decision-making charts to strengthen your position. You will be assessed for your presentation style and the strength of your argument. It is important that there are three distinct points of view. There will be peer assessment and teacher assessment.

Rumeeza, Vladia, and Susan believed that this Big Assessment task connected directly to the *know*. To demonstrate what they knew, students had to *do* basic research (researching); produce a map (mapping); analyze, synthesize, and evaluate data by applying a decision-making model (decision making); write a persuasive letter (writing); and present orally to an audience (oral communication). Finally, they needed to demonstrate interpersonal skills such as cooperation in their groups (*be*). The *be* would be evident in the way the students did the task. Were they cooperative? Independent?

How did Rumeeza, Vladia, and Susan plan for the daily activities? They integrated the activities and assessments and let the standards guide this process. Figure 5.16 shows the template that they used. The last column shows how each activity connected to the KDB and Big Assessment Task.

In this chapter, we explored how to create Big Questions to guide the unit. Big Questions were differentiated from topic questions. The connection between Big Questions and Big Understandings was made. We followed Lydia as she made her daily decisions for lessons that led to the KDB and her Big Assessment task. Then we looked at how educators planned for a Grade 7 integrated unit in a way that ensured the curriculum was aligned.

DISCUSSION QUESTIONS

1. Some educators prefer to develop Big Questions before the Big Assessment task. Why? What would work best for you in your context? Why?

2. Recall a unit that you experienced as a student or a teacher. If there were Big Questions, did they enhance the lessons? If not, what Big Questions might have improved the unit?

3. Discuss two-dimensional thinking. How is this different from traditional planning? What benefits can you see?

Figure 5.16   The Templates for the Daily Activities of the Red Hill Unit

Instructional Activity	Standards	Assessment Tasks/Tools	KDB Big Assessment
Field trip to Red Hill Creek (where a new highway is proposed) In groups, you will map one section of Red Hill Creek. Pictorial symbols will be used to represent major environmental features such as trees, weeds, birds, and insects. The sections will be used to create a class overview of the area. Using the community Data Sheet compile a list of species in the area you mapped. Use the list to join a discussion on how community members provide food and shelter for one another. Use the observation sheet to identify the changes made to the natural environment. Be ready to discuss in class.	Compile quantitative and qualitative data gathered through investigation. Use diagrams, flow charts, frequency tables (e.g., Use a chart to record numbers of producers and consumers in a particular habitat. (S, G) Identify living (biotic) and non-living (abiotic) elements in an ecosystem. (S) Identify populations of organisms within an ecosystem and factors that contribute to their survival. (S) Use appropriate vocabulary. (S, G, E) Demonstrate an understanding of the themes of geography, particularly movement and place. (G)	*Tasks:* Charts, Diagrams, maps/ *Tool:* Teacher marks for accuracy *Task* Discussion *Tool:* Teacher observation	This field trip shows students that real environmental issues are in their own community. This task integrates geography and science. Covers **Big Understandings** Plants and animals in a specific habitat are interdependent. Humans are a part of the natural environment and have an impact on it. **Big Ideas** Systems Interdependence Sustainability Research skills Interpersonal skills Mapping Systems thinking

Figure 5.16 (Continued)

Instructional Activity	Standards	Assessment Tasks/Tools	KDBbig Assessment
In a group, research a current environmental issue using the Internet and other sources. On a map, locate the area where your issue is occurring. Summarize important facts about this issue. Use a decision-making organizer to organize your ideas and help you to move toward a solution. (Think about the organizer from the Environmental Explorer as a starting place.)	Communicate an understanding that various individuals and groups have different opinions on this issue. (G) Analyse, synthesize, and evaluate data by applying a decision-making model to an environmental issue. (G) Produce maps for a variety of purposes. (G) Use the 5 themes of geography. (G)	*Task*: Research *Tool:* Teacher assessment of summary *Task:* Decision-making organizer *Tool:* Rubric Teacher and peer evaluation	This task builds on the last two by asking students now to locate an environmental issue anywhere in the world. The observations in the last two exercises should help to keep them aligned with the Big Understandings/ Big Ideas.
Individually, write a one-page letter to the editor of the local paper where your situation is located. Use the 5 themes from geography to express your opinion about this issue. Use a direct and persuasive style to try and get readers to agree with you. Edit your work individually and then in pairs.	Produce a report on a current environmental event. (G) Use knowledge of a variety of written forms to produce a piece of writing appropriate for the purpose and the audience. (E) Revise and edit their work focusing on content and style, independently and in collaboration with others. (E)	*Task:* Letter *Tool:* Rubric Pairs will evaluate revision and editing process. Teacher evaluation of final letter.	Students will need to express the relationships in the Big Understandings and show understanding of Big Ideas. Need to show cooperation for the editing process.

SOURCE: Adapted from Biodiversity Performs at http://worldwildlife.org/fun/games/ performs/biod-performs.pdf and Environmental Explorer http://www.nationalgeographic .com/ Vladia Jusko McBrian, Rumeeza Salim, and Susan McLachlin.

4. Why are two-dimensional thinking and principles of learning offered together as a way to plan the daily activities? What is the relationship between the two for you?

5. Think back to positive learning experiences in your life. What principles of learning were involved? Similarly, think of negative learning experiences. Can you extrapolate any learning principles from these experiences?

6. Explore Figure 5.7. How does this fit your previous learning experiences? How might these experiences have been different if this chart had been considered?

7. Review assessment *of, for*, and *as* learning in Chapter 4. How does this fit with Figure 5.7?

SUGGESTED ACTIVITIES

1. Review Figure 3.6 for examples of concepts that could be categorized as Big Ideas (interdisciplinary concepts). Choose two Big Ideas to work with. Using the formula for Big Questions, create a number of Big Questions with the two Big Ideas. Repeat the experience. How do the questions differ in quality?

2. Use the curriculum that you have been building from Chapter 3. Create two or three appropriate Big Questions to guide the daily learning experiences.

3. Using Figure 5.7, consider how assessment and instruction can be integrated with the standards to create some daily learning activities. Make sure that the activities and assessments align with the KDB and the Big Assessment task.

4. You have created several different assessments and activities. How well have you included assessment *of, for*, and *as* learning? To include these three types of assessment, what do you need to add or omit?

6

A Sample Interdisciplinary Curriculum Based on Standards

In this chapter, we put the pieces together to create an interdisciplinary curriculum. This task requires both two-dimensional and systems thinking. Each piece is connected to the other pieces, and they are interdependent with one another. The process is generic and can be applied to any grade level.

In this chapter, we view the work of Gail Higenell and Silvia Greco. They created a curriculum on fables. Although this particular example is at the Grade 4 level, the principles can be extrapolated and used in any context and at any level of education.

In Appendix A, there is a curriculum sample for Grade 10 using the same model. Also, there is a rubric/checkbric for designers to ensure the quality of the curriculum design (see Appendix B).

The steps for creating a standards-based curriculum are outlined here (see Table 6.1). They appear in a linear order, but because the steps are interconnected with the others, there are often overlaps and moving back and forth among the steps to confirm that connections are in place.

Table 6.1   Steps for Creating a Standards-Based Interdisciplinary Curriculum

Prestep 1:	Curriculum Map for connections.
Prestep 2:	Scan and Cluster the standards horizontally and vertically.
Step 1:	Choose an age-appropriate and relevant topic/theme.
Step 2:	Select appropriate broad-based standards.
Step 3:	Create an exploratory web.
Step 4:	Create a KDB Umbrella.
Step 5:	Create a Big Assessment task where students can demonstrate that they have achieved the KDB.
Step 6:	Create Big Questions.
Step 7:	Create mini-units to address the Big Questions.
Step 8:	Create the ongoing activities/assessments tasks based on the standards. Select appropriate assessment tools. Check that these ongoing activities/assessments are connected to the KDB and lead to Big Assessment task.

Gail Higenell (ghigenel@brocku.ca) and Silvia Greco (silvia.greco@dsbn.edu.on.ca) followed these steps to develop a standards-based inter-disciplinary curriculum.

Inevitably, teachers put their personal stamps on this generic process. You will see this in Gail and Silvia's work. As student-centered educators, Gail and Silvia wanted students to have input into the curriculum. Gail and Silvia intended ultimately to create the Big Questions with the students (Step 6). They began their planning with two questions that, in their experiences, were typical of the questions that Grade 4 students would ask. If their students created different questions, they would modify their ongoing activities and assessment tasks to address the student questions if necessary. However, regardless of the Big Questions, the ongoing assessments and activities must lead to the Big Assessment task and the Know/Do/Be (KDB) Umbrella.

Gail and Silvia were particularly interested in applying the multiple intelligences as a way to support student success. They saw the multiple intelligences as falling naturally into the activities and assessment tasks generated in the following subject areas:

- Language arts: Making lists, reading, writing, creating, recording, analyzing, graphing, comparing and contrasting, evaluating (linguistic)
- Math: Observing, measuring, duplicating, applying concepts (mathematical/logical)
- Social studies: Logging data, drawing, critical thinking (naturalist, mathematical/logical)
- Arts: Story boarding, observation, drawing, diagramming, performing, constructing, videotaping, photographing, listening, playing,

composing, audiotaping, selecting, critiquing (visual, spatial, musical, bodily/kinesthetic)

- Physical education: Cooperating, improvising, collaborating, compromising, using creative movement, following instructions (bodily/kinesthetic, visual, spatial).
- Cross-disciplinary: Discussing, responding, reporting, questioning, working together (interpersonal); intuiting, reflecting, rehearsing, self-assessing, preparing (intrapersonal)

In the last column in Step 8, the intelligences they included are written in italics. The multiple intelligences ensured that the curriculum reached all types of learners. Also, the daily activities and assessment tasks completed the unit and led to the KDB and the culminating activity. Silvia and Gail stressed that all activities acted as assessments of some sort. These activities/assessments also connected to the standards and were often rooted in them.

PRESTEPS

Gail and Silvia began with a Scan and Cluster of the curriculum. Because they were educators in two separate institutions in Ontario, they did not complete curriculum maps. The Scan and Cluster allowed them a good overview of the curriculum. They decided to include language arts, math, physical education, the arts, and social studies. By emphasizing the multiple intelligences, they would cover a lot of the arts curriculum. It also meant that they would need to teach the skills to produce the products in the arts.

STEP 1: CHOOSE AN AGE-APPROPRIATE AND RELEVANT TOPIC THEME

Fables

STEP 2: SELECT APPROPRIATE BROAD-BASED STANDARDS

Gail and Silvia selected these standards from the Ontario Grade 4 curriculum documents (http://www.edu.gov.on.ca, 1998).

- Communicate ideas and information for a variety of purposes and to specific audiences (language, 1997).
- Produce two- and three-dimensional works of art that communicate ideas for specific purposes and to specific audiences (visual arts, 1998).
- Use appropriate strategies to organize and carry out group projects such as brainstorming, summarizing, reporting, and giving and following instructions (language, 1997).

- Communicate their response to music in ways appropriate for this grade (arts, 1998).
- Interpret and communicate the meaning of stories, poems, plays, and other material drawn from a variety of sources and cultures, using a variety of drama and dance techniques (arts, 1998).
- Investigate the attributes of three-dimensional figures and two-dimensional shapes using concrete materials and drawings (math, 1997).
- Apply decision-making and problem-solving skills in addressing threats to personal safety, such as abuse, physical fighting, and injury prevention (physical education and health, 1998).
- Apply life skills such as goal setting, conflict-resolution techniques, and interpersonal skills (e.g., playing fairly, cooperating, behaving respectfully) to physical activities (physical education and health, 1998).
- Construct and read a wide variety of graphs, charts, diagrams, maps, and models for specific purposes (social studies, 1998).

STEP 3: CREATE AN EXPLORATORY WEB

Figure 6.1   An Exploratory Web for "Fables"

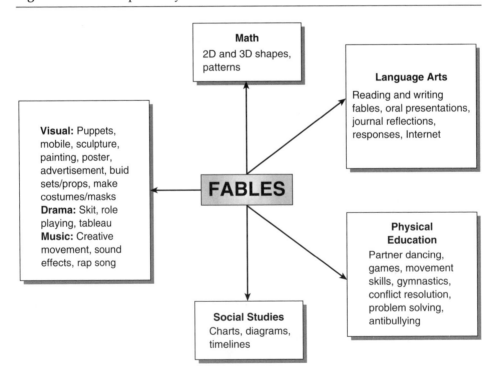

SOURCE: Gail Higenell and Silvia Greco.

STEP 4: CREATE A KDB UMBRELLA

Figure 6.2   The Know/Do/Be Umbrella for "Fables"

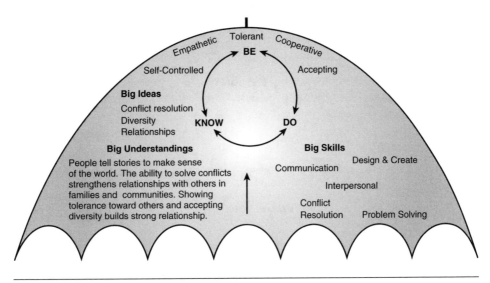

SOURCE: Based on the work of Gail Higenell and Silvia Greco.

STEP 5: CREATE A BIG ASSESSMENT TASK IN WHICH STUDENTS CAN DEMONSTRATE THAT THEY HAVE ACHIEVED THE KDB (TABLE 6.2)

Table 6.2   The Big Assessment Task for "Fables"

The Peaceable Kingdom

Your Grade Four class will host a peace exhibition called The Peaceable Kingdom. At this exhibition, your visitors will learn about conflict resolution and responsibilities of community members to develop tolerance and accept differences in others in order to build strong relationships. Parents, other classes, teachers, and other guests will be visitors. There will be stations setup in the gym. Each station represents an important ingredient for a Peaceable Kingdom.

1. You and your three partners will be at one station.

- Using the fable book you created in class, act out the story. You may do this as a puppet play using the puppets you created, or you may be the actors.

(Continued)

Table 6.2 (Continued)

- Using a variety of media, design and create your own costumes/masks or puppets to star in your fable.

- Build your own set with props, background posters/set boards or puppet house. Include as many visual effects as you can that represent animals in the wild and a natural environment. Use as many art products as you can from the ones you created during our unit.

- Locate three musical pieces from the library or compose your own and weave this music as well as other appropriate sound effects throughout your play at the appropriate places.

2. Organize a kiosk around your station.

- Create a colorful and creative banner announcing the title of your fable and listing your names.

- Be prepared to display and discuss your written and illustrated story in book form.

- On a poster board, use a diagram to chart the problem solving model you used to resolve the conflict in your fable.

- Prove how it worked.

- Propose an alternative to the behaviors in the story that might have prevented the problem from escalating.

- In chart form, compare and contrast the characters, demonstrating the personality problems of the characters that led to the problem.

- Explain in writing, as well as orally, as groups come to your kiosk, the moral of your story and justify how you arrived at that lesson.

- Rationalize why it is an important and valuable lesson for others to learn. Include photographs or a video of you and your group, which demonstrates how you built and created your sets, props, and costumes or puppets.

There will be teacher, peer and self-assessment of your visual and oral presentation, for an overall understanding of the Big Ideas of conflict resolution and resolving differences in a community. Presentation skills will also be evaluated. All of the tasks necessary to complete this Big Assessment Task will be evaluated as you accomplish them.

STEP 6: CREATE BIG QUESTIONS

Why is it important for people to tell stories?

How can we develop relationships with people who differ from us?

STEP 7: CREATE MINI-UNITS TO ADDRESS THE BIG QUESTIONS

Recluster the standards, assessments, and activities in the exploratory web to do this. Sometimes the units directly answer the Big Questions. Gail and Silvia chose to do this. At other times, the Big Questions may guide the entire unit and the mini-units, while the mini-units focus on a smaller theme. This is shown in Figure 6.3.

Figure 6.3   Mini-Unit Planning for "Fables"

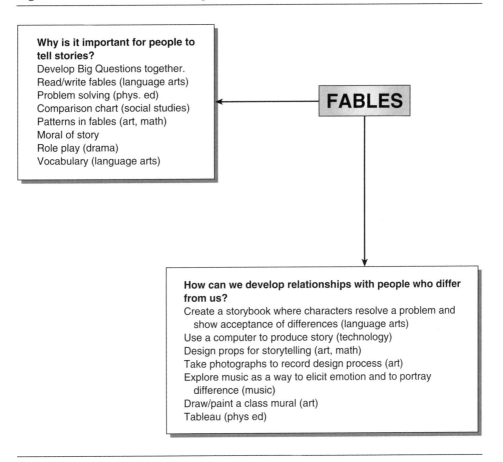

SOURCE: Gail Higenell and Silvia Greco.

STEP 8: CREATE THE ONGOING ACTIVITIES AND ASSESSMENTS BASED ON THE STANDARDS

Select assessment tools. Check that these are connected to the KDB and lead to the Big Assessment task. Gail and Silvia's planning for the first Big Question is in Figure 6.4.

(Text continues on page 131)

Figure 6.4 Mini-Unit for "Why Is It Important to Tell Stories?"

Why is it important to tell stories?			
Instructional Activities	**Assessment Tasks**	**Standards**	**KDB/ Big Assessment Task**
Introduce fables with a motivator-movie depicting some fables (Fables of the Green Forest). Set up a fables book display. Discuss some of the ways the characters treat each other. Introduce new vocabulary (e.g., personality, characteristics). Personalize this by having students describe themselves and others, and by attributing specific characteristics to the characters in the fables. On the board, make a comparison chart. Discuss the pattern of elements in fables (e.g., a moral, animals, etc.).

Develop Big Questions together
(Interpersonal, Intrapersonal) | Task: Discussion
Tool: Teacher observation on participation and the students' ability to extract meaning from a listening experience.

Task: Class development of chart
Tool: Anecdotal notes

Task: Develop Big Questions
Tool: N/A | Oral & Visual Communication:
4e54 communicate a main idea about a topic and describe a short sequence of events
4e53 ask questions on a variety of topics and respond appropriately to the questions of others
4e59 analyze media works
4e52 communicate various types of messages, explain some ideas and procedures, and follow the teacher's instructions
4e66 listen to others and stay on topic in group discussion
Social Studies:
Construct and read a chart | Leads to an understanding of stories as ways to make meaning and solve problems. Introduce conflict resolution and diversity. In this context, discuss Big Understandings: Roles and responsibilities to self, family, and communities.
Prepare for patterns in stories and writing a story. |

Why is it important to tell stories?			
Instructional Activities	**Assessment Tasks**	**Standards**	**KDB/ Big Assessment Task**
Problem Solving: Present some other fables without the endings on overhead. (Shared reading.) Preteach any new vocabulary. (Some of these words can be listed for spelling words later.) Brainstorm possible endings. Discuss the steps for effective problem solving. Role-play these endings, demonstrating clever ways to avoid problems, using a problem-solving model, and then including original elements and their own feelings to influence the ending (creativity, flexibility, curiosity, confidence). Discuss how to make a role play seem "real" through the use of voice, expression, facial gestures, etc. Show them a picture of the Peaceable Kingdom and discuss what makes for a peaceable kingdom. *(Mathematical/Logical, Bodily/Kinesthetic, Linguistic)*	Task: Reading and brainstorm endings. Discuss possible endings. Effective problem-solving steps. Tool: Teacher observation Task: Role play. Use problem-solving model Tool: Peer assessment, teacher and self-evaluation Students generate a checklist as a class with the teacher and a rating scale 1–3, including their impressions of what makes a good role play. Students rate themselves based on their own criteria. Students also rate each other on their role plays and on their ability to follow the problem-solving model effectively.	Reading: 4e28 read aloud, speaking clearly and with expression 4e30 state their own interpretation of a written work, using evidence from the work and from their own knowledge and experience 4e38 make predictions while reading 4e39 retell a story by adapting it for presentation in another way 4e40 develop their own opinions by reading Oral Communication: 4e66 listen to others and stay on topic in group discussion Drama: 4a50 interpret and communicate the meaning of stories, poems, plays, and other material [...] using a variety of drama techniques 4a54 demonstrate an understanding of voice and audience by speaking and writing in role as characters in a story 4a68 identify their own feelings and reactions, and compare them with those of a character Health & Phys. Ed. 4p8 identify the characteristics of healthy relationships (e.g., showing consideration of others' feelings by avoiding negative communication) 4p9 identify the challenges (e.g., conflicting opinions) and responsibilities in their relationships with family and friends	Students see variations in stories and why and how they are effective. Enables them to write their own stories. Role playing is needed for the final Big Assessment Task.

SOURCE: Gail Higenell and Silvia Greco.

Figure 6.5 Mini-Unit for "How Can We Develop Relationships With People Who Differ From Us?"

How can we develop relationships with people who differ from us?

Instructional Activities	Assessment Tasks	Standards	KDB/ Big Assessment Task
Students work collaboratively in groups of four to read and share four other fables not read in class. Together they explore the characters and situations and identify patterns they notice lead to conflict, as well as the elements (format) of fables. The group writes and illustrates an original fable using a storybook word processor program on the computer. They create their own characters (at least 4) that show unique characteristics. Each fable must include a social skills problem, teamwork, relationships, and differences. They must apply one of the problem-solving strategies to their fable and have their characters work through those steps to solve the problem. *(Linguistic, Interpersonal, Intrapersonal, Mathematical/Logical)*	Task: Reading. Identify patterns of conflict. Tool: Teacher observation Task: Write a storybook in groups. Use the computer to write. Illustrate the storybook. Edit their stories. Tools: Rubric for story and drawing. Teacher evaluation. Anecdotal notes for computer skills. Self- editing and peer editing checklist Task: Oral presentation of the patterns of the elements in their fables and patterns of actions that lead to conflict. Tool: Presentation rubric (teacher evaluation) Task: Cooperative learning Tool: Checklists/rubrics to evaluate collaboration Task: Listening skills Tools: Peer assessment and teacher assessment.	Reading: 4e29 read independently, using a variety of reading strategies 4e35 identify and describe elements of stories Health & Physical Education: 4p9identify the challenges (e.g., conflicting opinions) and responsibilities in their relationships with family and friends Art: Writing: 4e5 produce pieces of writing using a variety of specific forms and materials from other media to enhance their writing 4e7 revise and edit their work using feedback from the teacher and peers 4e8 proofread and correct their final drafts focusing on grammar, punctuation, and spelling (Almost all other writing expectations can be addressed with these activities.) Oral Communication: 4e65 present information to their peers in a focused and organized form on a topic of mutual interest 4e66 listen to others and stay on topic/group discussion 4e67 use appropriate strategies to organize and carry out group projects (e.g., brainstorming, summarizing, reporting, giving and following instructions)	Create the storybook for Big Assessment Task. Work with problem solving and conflict resolution dealing with diversity. Collaboration requires acceptance of difference as a responsibility of being a community member.

How can we develop relationships with people who differ from us?

Instructional Activities	Assessment Tasks	Standards	KDB/ Big Assessment Task
Teach the skills to design and construct masks, costumes, banners, props, and character puppets. Each group to take 4–10 photographs of what they consider to be some valuable points in their classmates' progress. Products must capture the feeling, mood, and personality of the characters created in their stories. *(Visual/Spatial, Mathematical/Logical, Interpersonal, Intrapersonal, Naturalist)*	<u>Task</u>: Create masks, costumes, banners, props, and character puppets <u>Tool</u>: Art rubric. The rubric includes evaluation on how effectively the products depict the feelings of characters. <u>Task</u>: Each group to take 4–10 photographs of what they consider to be some valuable points in their classmates' progress. <u>Tool</u>: checklist for criteria for photo shots <u>Task</u>: Collaborate in group <u>Tool</u>: Group collaboration rubric Self-evaluation Peer evaluation <u>Task</u>: Investigate attributes of 2- and 3-dimensional figures <u>Tool</u>: Math rubric-teacher assessment	<u>Oral Communication (Media skills)</u>: 4368 identify camera angles and distance from the subject in photographs and describe their effects on the viewer's perceptions <u>Math</u>: 4m62 investigate the attributes of three-dimensional figures and two-dimensional shapes using concrete materials and drawings 4m68 identify the two-dimensional shapes of the faces of three-dimensional figures 4m69 sketch the faces that make up a three-dimensional figure using concrete materials as models 4m70 design and make skeletons (e.g., with straws or toothpicks and marshmallows for three-dimensional figures) <u>Visual Arts</u>: 4a43 produce two-and three-dimensional works of art (i.e., works involving media and techniques used in drawing, painting, sculpting; printmaking) that communicate thoughts, feelings, and ideas for specific purposes and to specific audiences	Create the products needed for Big Assessment Task. Awareness of feeling mood and personalities diversity and conflict resolution. Collaboration requires acceptance of difference as a responsibility of being a community member.

(Continued)

129

Figure 6.5 (Continued)

130

How can we develop relationships with people who differ from us?			
Instructional Activities	**Assessment Tasks**	**Standards**	**KDB/ Big Assessment Task**
Show the movie *Peter and the Wolf*. Focus on sound effects. Introduce instruments and allow students to create different sound effects that depict moods. Discuss how music elicits different feelings and thoughts among people, creating differences in the way people experience emotions and feelings. Explore classical music and use various excerpts to represent a particular animal and the personality of that animal. Students make a class mural of an animal kingdom, drawing and painting inspired by the music. Students videotape different segments of the instrument-playing activities, as well as the process of working on the class mural. *(Visual/Spatial, Musical, Bodily/Kinesthetic, Interpersonal, Intrapersonal, Naturalist, Linguistic)*	Task: Discussion Tool: Teacher observation and anecdotal recording Task: Student instrument performances Tool: Music rubric for their self, peer and teacher assessment Task: Videotaping Tool: Rubric for video assessment Teacher observation and anecdotal notes Task: Class mural Tool: Art rubric assessment Task: Collaborate with group Tool: Collaboration assessment	Music: 4a1 demonstrate an understanding of the basic elements of music specified for this grade through listening to, performing, and creating music 4a2 create and perform music, using a variety of sound sources 4a6 communicate their response to music in ways appropriate for this grade (e.g., through visual arts, drama, creative movement, language) 4a29 describe how a composer can manipulate the elements of music to create a specific mood (e.g., in The Sorcerer's Apprentice by Kukas) 4a30 explain the effects of different musical choices Visual Arts: 4a36 identify the emotional quality of lines (e.g., smooth, flowing, horizontal lines create a feeling of peace and harmony; sharp, jagged, vertical lines create a feeling of energy and unease) 4a43 produce two- and three-dimensional works of art that communicate thoughts, feelings, and ideas for specific purposes and to specific audiences Oral Communication (Media Skills): 4e68 create a variety of media works	Create the music for Big Assessment Task. Be aware of emotions and feeling and what engenders negative feelings. Collaboration requires acceptance of difference as a responsibility of being a community member.

SOURCE: Gail Higenell and Silvia Greco.

(Text continued from page 125)

In this chapter, we have seen an example of a standards-based interdisciplinary curriculum. It is based on the procedures described in Chapters 1, 3, 4, and 5. In the next two chapters, we will explore how others have addressed bridging accountability and relevance when designing an integrated curriculum.

DISCUSSION QUESTIONS

1. "Fables" is a unit created by Gail and Silvia. It is not a perfect unit. Critique the unit using the rubric in Appendix B. In particular, comment on the alignment in the unit.

2. Review the daily lesson activities. Critique how well Gail and Silvia have embedded assessment into the activities and how well they match the standards. Can you think of other assessment tools that would work?

3. Discuss how well Gail and Silvia have used two-dimensional thinking (Figure 5.6). How well do the daily activities and assessments fit the KDB and the Big Assessment task?

4. The authors of this unit used the template of multiple intelligences as a way to ensure variety in their activities. Multiple intelligences include linguistic, mathematical/logical, naturalistic, bodily/kinesthetic, spatial, interpersonal, intrapersonal, and musical intelligences. Discuss how well they have done this. How would this curriculum have been different if they had not consciously used this template?

5. How well do the intended assessment tools fit the assessment tasks in the daily activities?

SUGGESTED ACTIVITIES

1. If you have done the activities in the previous chapters, you have completed much of the work to create a relevant interdisciplinary unit. Using the example offered in this chapter and in Appendix A, refine the curriculum that you have been working on. If you are just starting, create your own integrated curriculum at the level that is relevant to you following the steps outlined in this chapter and in the Appendix.

2. A rubric/checkbric has been provided in Appendix B. Glynnis Fleming is a resource teacher who developed this tool for student teachers. Some of the tool is in rubric form. Some of it is a checklist for both her and the student teachers to use while they discuss their process and product with her. Discuss how you could use this tool and then use it.

7

Exploring Other Interdisciplinary and Integrated Models

In this book, we have the explored the fundamentals for creating a sound curriculum that is standards based. Many of the strategies that have been promoted are helpful when developing any curriculum, whether it is disciplinary or interdisciplinary. Once the basics are in place, there is a wide variety of ways to design curriculum. This chapter explores some of these ways. In the last three examples, the students are progressively more involved in some or all of the planning for the unit.

THE CURRY/SAMARA MODEL

James Curry and John Samara have developed a standards-based curriculum model that has stood the test of time. Research indicates statistically significant results in terms of academic improvement on standardized tests, especially in low-socioeconomic environments over an eight-year period (see, for example, Connell, 2003; Curry, Samara, & Connell, 2005; Henderson, 2000). Details of extensive research on the Curriculum Project are available at http://www.curriculumproject.com.

Grounded in this philosophy, teachers can begin to plan units. The CSM unit matrix is the heart of the Curry/Samara Model (Figure 7.1).

Figure 7.1   The Curry/Samara Model Unit Matrix

Rain Forests	Basic Thinking ⟶	
	Knowledge	**Comprehension**

1. Characteristics
  ❑ Locations
  ❑ Landforms
  ❑ Waterways
  ❑ Layers
  ❑ Climate
	1. Identify the absolute and relative locations of a rain forest.
	
	*Word map/Bullet chart
		2. Describe the landforms found in the rain forest.
		
		*Dictionary entries

2. Life in the Rain Forest
  ❑ Plants
  ❑ Animals
  ❑ Humans
  ❑ Interdependence
	7. Recall the animals and plants most commonly found in the rain forest.
	
	*Word search
		8. Explain the relationship among plants, animals, and humans.
		
		*Cycle diagram Written explanat'n

3. Products from Rain Forests
  ❑ Chemical
  ❑ Medicinal
  ❑ Wood products
  ❑ Foods
	13. Recount chemical, medicinal, , and food products that originate in the rain forest.
	
	*Dictionary entries
		14. Describe the phases through which any rain forest product will evolve when going to market.
		
		*Timeline

4. Rain Forests Issues
  ❑ Deforestation
  ❑ Soil erosion
  ❑ Endangered species
	19. Restate the names and locations of endangered animal species.
	
	*Map puzzle
		20. Describe the cycle of soil erosion.
		
		*Diagram/Oral presentation

5. Patterns
  ❑ Consist of repeating segments
  ❑ allow for prediction
  ❑ Can be man-made or natural
	25. Identify the repeating segments of a natural cycle in the rain forest.
	
	*Role play
		26. Describe man-made and natural patterns in the rain forest.
		
		*Class discussion/ Charts

INDEPENDENT STUDY	Select a Topic	Develop a Challenge

Abstract Thinking →

Application	Analysis	Creative Thinking	Critical Thinking
3. Model the floor, understudy, canopy, and emergent layers of a rain forest. *Class mural	4. Examine the importance of rain forest rivers. *Magazine article	5. Change a rain forest's location and explain the effects on plants and animals. *Descriptive essay	6. Decide which layer of the rain forest is best suited for human habitation. *Illustrated poem
9. Categorize animals according to the rain forest layers in which they live. *Animal puzzle	10. Compare/ contrast two kinds of animals from the same layer of the rain forest. *T-chart	11. Develop a plant, animal, or person that is suited to live in the rain forest. *Videotaped documentary	12. Defend/dispute the concept of protecting a selected plant or animal species. *Debate
15. Classify various rain forest products into self-generated categories. *Classification puzzle	16. Determine which rain forest products are consumed in the local community. *Research presentation	17. Invent a habitat in which medicine might be produced. *Labeled diagram	18. Decide on environmentally sound ways of harvesting a selected product. *Letter to the editor
21. Categorize endangered species by reasons of endangerment. *Information table	22. Determine how deforestation impacts habitats within the rain forest. *Board game	23. Speculate how overconsumption of rain forest products might be reduced. *Campaign speech	24. Defend/ dispute a selected law that protects endangered species. *Point-of-view essay
27. Categorize rain forest patterns as natural or man-made. *Venn Diagram	28. Examine the patterns of two products that originate in the rain forest. *Brochure	29. Generate an original natural or man-made pattern that would help the rain forest. *Illustrated poem	30. Decide which natural pattern within the rain forest is impacted most by man. *Persuasive speech
Develop a Plan	Gather Information	Organize Information	Present the Findings

Curry and Samara have created a model that is at once simple and complex. At its best, it is a sophisticated model that seems to cover all the bases from a constructivist teaching perspective. They begin with applying best practices to create relevant learning activities. Each curriculum unit has four building blocks: content, thinking skills, product, and independent study (research). The details for these building blocks are in Figure 7.2.

Teachers begin with the standards. The alignment of curriculum is achieved through filling in the cells of the matrix. Content (*know*) moves from factual to global and is conceptual in nature. Curry and Samara have adapted Bloom's taxonomy to determine the skills (*do*) ranging from the concrete to the abstract: knowledge, comprehension, application, analysis, creative thinking, and critical thinking.

Figure 7.2   The Dimensions of Curriculum, Instruction, and Assessment

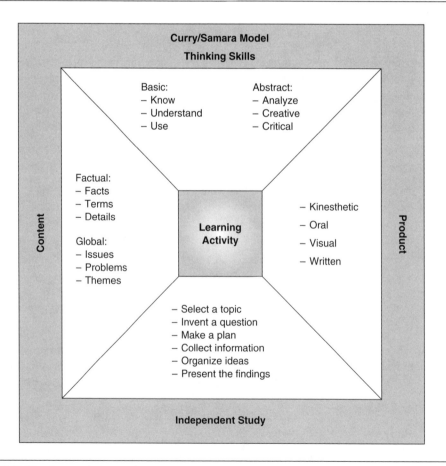

SOURCE: Copyright 1998 by J. Curry and J. Samara. The Curriculum Project. www .curriculumproject.com.

Curry and Samara show a deep understanding of the interdisciplinary nature of assessment tasks and their relationship to developing an interdisciplinary curriculum. A supporting software tool helps teachers plan curriculum tasks and choose from a wide variety of relevant products for students to demonstrate their learning. The products are generic and interdisciplinary, ranging from essays, diagrams, and oral reports to creating models. A generic assessment tool accompanies the assessment task (product).

Accountability is central to this project. Teachers who adopt the CSM will inevitably be thinking about teaching in new ways. They are supported through the process through an initial staff development session, ongoing study group meetings, brief administrator walk-throughs, and visitations by someone outside the school.

BOX 7.1

USING THE CSM MATRIX

The following steps are necessary to fill in the matrix (Figure 7.1):

1. The theme of the unit is determined first, and usually, this is derived directly from the standards.

2. The teacher reviews the standards to determine what is important for a student to know and be able to do.

3. The content is organized in the cells in the left-hand side of the matrix. Using the standards as a guide, the teacher organizes the content in these cells moving from lower-order concepts (facts) to higher-order or more global forms of knowledge such as issues, problems, and themes.

4. In the CSM, the thinking skills are located along the top axis of the matrix and organized from the lower-order skills to the higher-order ones. The standards are reviewed for an overview of which skills are required. In this model, activities for all skills from the identification of knowledge to critical thinking need to be designed regardless of curriculum mandates.

5. The instructional activities can now be designed to fill in the matrix cells. The formula for a well-written cell entry is as follows: a cognitive verb + content at the appropriate conceptual level + a product. Essentially this means that the *know* and *do* and assessment are described in concrete terms.

6. Lesson plans are created to accompany the cell entry. A template is available. A lesson plan is not required for every cell. See Figure 7.3.

7. Product guides are created to complement lesson plans. The product guide outlines the criteria necessary to create an excellent product. These guides are interdisciplinary and can be used in any area of study.

(Continued)

Box 7.1 (Continued)

> They can also be adapted into rubrics and used for assessment purposes. Product guides are available for such things as a dramatization, model, simulation, debate, collection, demonstration, and a skit. An example of a product guide for a timeline is offered in Figure 7.4.
>
> 8. The learning objective is posted daily in the classroom to provide students with a clear description of expectations. Students may also be a part of developing product guides.

Also, there is an emphasis on student use of technology. The specific use of technology is often integrated into the directions for the student to create a product. For example, a task in one cell may read: "Identify the percentages of selected ethnic groups that fought in the Texas Revolution after searching the CD encyclopedia—Circle Graph" (desktop presentation software). Examples of ways to integrate technology into instructional activities are offered in Figure 7.5.

INTEGRATING TECHNOLOGY INTO THE CURRICULUM WITH A WEBQUEST

Marci Steele has been teaching for nine years. This is in her sixth year teaching Grade 2 at Milton J. Brecht Elementary School in Lancaster, PA. It is a small, suburban school with an average of two classes per grade level. Students are of multiethnic origins and have multiple socioeconomic backgrounds.

Currently, Marci is the technology liaison for her building. She also is involved in the district's technology mentor program. She works with several teachers each year on developing lessons and projects that integrate technology into the existing curriculum. Marci has noticed that when content areas are linked to each other, the students seem to be more engaged and show more motivation toward the lessons and activities. The students have a higher interest in the subject.

Figure 7.6 shows a Webquest that Marci created as a part of a larger unit called "Soils." The Grade 2 students loved it because they used the school's laptops. Individually, the students had to create a compost from scratch and had to search through the Webquest for the process of how to make one. They came away with a deeper understanding of the environmental aspect of the Soils unit than previous classes that had not done a Webquest and had created one large compost as a class. The students became very involved in this Webquest, and Marci found that she could be truly "hands off" and just monitor the class.

Marci integrates technology into the curriculum to create interest for the students, as well as for the exposure to and use of technology. Our society

Figure 7.3 Lesson Plan Template

Lesson Plan Template

Dimensions of Curriculum
    Content/Subject Matter
    Thinking Skill
    Student Products

Student Learning Objective
    In their study of:
    Students will:
    And share their ideas using:

Description of Activity
    The Teacher will:

    1. Engage students with the subject matter by . . .

    2. Explain and/or label the type of thinking required for the activity by . . .

    3. Describe the product(s) that will be used by . . .

    4. Discuss specific standards of excellence for this activity.

    5. Assist students as they work.

    6. Summarize the major points of the activity.

Materials
    Necessary materials that are not usually found in the classroom.

Environment
    Learning environment(s) for this activity.

Standards
    The objectives that match this lesson.

SOURCE: Copyright 1998 by J. Curry and J. Samara. The Curriculum Project. www .curriculumproject.com.

makes constant use of technology, and this generation needs to be adept in using it. She also thinks that teaching through a Webquest is a constructivist teaching approach. Students engaging in the Webquest need to do more than just "spit out" the facts. Students need to problem solve and think through the project. Given that there is so much information available today, higher-order thinking skills are necessary so that students can manage information, and these skills can be transferred from one situation to another. The Webquest challenges students to engage in higher-order thinking (see Figure 7.7).

Figure 7.4   Product Guide for a Timeline

Timeline—Visual	
Parts	**Attributes**
Title	Prominent, concise, summarizes
Line	Ruled, may represent topic, arrowed
Time Increments	Uniform size per unit of time, clearly visible, equal intervals, subunits of time for important events
Labels	Printed legibly, uniform size, represents key events
Illustrations	Limited, highlights key events/concepts
Background	Nonobtrusive, may support main concept
Credits	Discrete, alphabetized, visible from front
Negative Space	Surrounds text, graphics, and boundaries of product

SOURCE: Copyright 1998 by J. Curry and J. Samara. The Curriculum Project. www
.curriculumproject.com.

Figure 7.5   Possible Ways to Integrate Technology Into the Curriculum

Integrating Technology With Knowledge Acquisition & With Student Products	
Task	**Technology**
Presentation	Presentation Software Concept Mapping Software
Research	Internet CD-ROM
Illustrated Poem	Paint Program Photo Editing Software
Report	Word Processor
Videotaped Documentary	MovieMaker or iMovie
Letter to the Editor	E-Mail

Figure 7.6   Integrating Technology Into a Curriculum Using a Webquest

---

A Home for Wesley Worm

A Webquest on Worms and the Environment

Designed by Marci E. Steele

Marci_steele@mtwp.net

Introduction

Wesley Worm has a problem. He doesn't have a home. He's traveled the world trying to find the perfect place. He's slept in a seashell, too gritty. He's floated on a puddle, too wet. He's even tried a boot, too smelly. That's where you come in! Now you must become a helminthologist (one who studies worms) so that you can create a home for Wesley Worm.

Task

Your job is to create a home for Wesley Worm. You will work with a team of helminthologists to collect all the information that you possibly can about worms and their homes. Then you will create an appropriate habitat for a worm. You will need to use the Internet links that your teacher provides to gather information about worms and their habitats. Along the way, you will record your information on data sheets and keep these in your Worm Folder. You will need to find out about the parts of a worm's body, the habitat of a worm, what a worm eats, why we need worms, and how to make a home for a worm. You will then use your new-found knowledge to create a home for Wesley, called a compost. You will make a miniature compost in a container right in your classroom and will put your very own Wesley Worm into his home. You and your teacher will supply a variety of materials from which to choose items for his home. After your experience, you will write a report on Wesley's future in his compost. When your project is complete, Wesley will move into our school garden.

Process

- First, your teacher will assign you to a group of 3 helminthologists and will give you a Worm Folder.

- Next, decide who will research these three areas. Click on and print these worksheets:

  - Worm Anatomy (body parts)

  - Worms in Nature/Soil Information

  - Composting

(Continued)

Figure 7.6 (Continued)

Print out the <u>Rubric</u> under the Evaluation section. This will let you know how you will be graded. Now answer the questions on the worksheets. You will need to visit the sites in the <u>Resources</u> section to get your information. Remember, you are a team. If one of your teamates needs some help, please do so. When you finish your worksheets, you will meet with your team of helminthologists and "teach" each other what you have learned. Put your worksheets into your Worm Folder so your teacher can grade them. Based on what you have just learned, now your team will plan how to make a compost for Wesley. Print these worksheets to help you plan. Decide what materials you will need and where you can get those materials. You may use things from home.

Compost Planning

Compost Materials

When you have planned your home for Wesley, get a compost container from your teacher and get the materials that you need and planned for.

Build Wesley's home. Use your planning worksheet to guide you.

Ask your teacher for a Wesley Worm. When you're ready, Wesley can move into his home.

Now write a report about Wesley's new life 2 months from now. Each teammate must write a report on his or her own. Make sure you answer all of the questions on your report form. Click here and print out the report form. When you're finished, put it in your Worm Folder to be graded.

Report Form

Resources

Click on these links to take you to Web sites that will help you answer your questions on your worksheet. You may need to check out each site until you find the answers you're looking for.

✐ <u>Yucky Worm World</u>
    (http://yucky.kids.discovery.com/noflash/worm/)

✐ <u>The Adventures of Herman the Worm</u>
    (http://www.urbanext.uiuc.edu/worms/)

✐ <u>Composting for Kids</u> (http://aggie-
    horticulture.tamu.edu/sustainable/slidesets/kidscompost/co ver.html)

✎ The Great Plant Escape
        (http://www.urbanext.uiuc.edu/gpe/case2/case2.html)

Evaluation

Students will be evaluated on the process (worksheets), the product (compost), and the analysis (report).

Click here to see a rubric.

Conclusion

Well done, helminthologists! You have successfully made a home for Wesley Worm. Now he can have a comfortable place to sleep and plenty of food to eat. In doing so, you have learned what a worm's body is like, what they eat, where they live, what a compost is, and how it is good for our world. Now you can continue taking care of your world and Wesley's. Go back and visit the sites in our Resources section to learn more and have fun! Consider making your own compost bin at your house with your parents' help.

Web sites to help you:

✎ Worm World/The Burrow
        (http://www.jetcompost.com/burrow/index.html)

✎ Worm Woman
        (http://www.wormwoman.com/acatalog/index.html)

✎ Worm Links
        (http://www.urbanext.uiuc.edu/worms/wormlinks/)

Books to read:

Diary of a Worm by Doreen Cronin

Worms Wiggle by David Pelham

Worms Eat My Garbage: How to Set Up and Maintain a Worm Composting System by Mary Appelhof

SOURCE: Marci Ervin Steele, Milton J. Brecht Elementary School, Lancaster, PA.

Figure 7.7   A Rubric for the Webquest

Rubric for Worm Webquest				
	Below Basic	**Basic**	**Proficient**	**Advanced**
Teamwork (Observable)	Student was uncooperative and always off task. Student did not participate in the team's project. Student had 4 or more complaints about him/her brought to the teacher.	Student sometimes cooperated with the team and sometimes stayed on task. Student had 3 complaints about him/her brought to the teacher.	Student cooperated with the team and stayed on task most of the time. Student has 1 or 2 complaints about him/her brought to the teacher.	Student cooperated with the team and stayed on task at all times. Student was an active participant. Student had no complaints about him/her brought to the teacher.
Worm Folder Worksheet	Student had an incomplete worksheet and/or worksheet had 5 or more mistakes.	Student completed the worksheet but had 3 or 4 mistakes in content.	Student completed the worksheet with 1 or 2 of the facts being inaccurate.	Student completed all parts of the worksheet. All facts on the worksheet were accurate.
Compost	Student did not produce a compost or had less than 75% organic materials in the compost and could not be used in the school garden or other natural environment.	Student produced a compost with 75% organic materials and it could not be used in the school garden or other natural environment.	Student produced a compost with 90% organic materials and could not be used in the school garden or other natural environment.	Student produced a perfect compost with 100% organic materials. Student's compost can be reused in the school garden or other natural environment.
Report	Student did not answer all questions in their final report and/or answers 3 or more incorrectly.	Student stays only with the facts and does not answer all of the questions and/or answers 1–2 questions incorrectly.	Student stays with the facts but does not go beyond. Student answers all questions accurately.	Student answered all questions in their final report accurately. Student went beyond the facts with detailed interpretation, personal insight.

SOURCE: Marci Ervin Steele, Milton J. Brecht Elementary School, Lancaster, PA.

Marci included a teachers' page in her Webquest. The information follows:

BOX 7.2
Teacher Notes

Objectives:

For students in Grade 2. This Webquest was designed to follow the Soils science kit by Science and Technology for Children®. Students will have basic background knowledge of soil parts before beginning this task.

Students will identify the parts of a worm's body.

Students will be able to explain how worms help our environment.

Students will be able to create a usable compost.

Students will explain what happens to a compost over time.

Pennsylvania Standards:

Science and Technology

3.1 Unifying Themes

   Illustrate patterns that regularly occur and reoccur in nature

   Recognize that change in natural systems

3.2 Inquiry and Design

   Identify and use the nature of scientific and technological knowledge

   Describe objects in the world using the five senses

   Recognize and use the elements of scientific inquiry to solve problems

   Recognize and use the technological design process to solve problems

3.3 Biological Sciences

   Know the similarities and differences of living things

   Know that living things are made up of parts that have specific functions

   Identify changes in living things over time

(Continued)

Box 7.2 (Continued)

Language Arts

1.2 Reading Critically in All Content Areas

Read and understand essential content of informational texts and documents in all academic areas

Use electronic media for research

1.8 Research

Locate information using appropriate sources and strategies

Organize and present the main ideas from research

Teacher Help and Hints:

Group students into heterogeneous groupings. Students should have previous experience with Internet searches and research.

There are several Word documents in this Webquest. If you would like it to open directly in your browser, please check your settings. Otherwise, they may download directly to the desktop.

Materials:

Use the largest plastic Ziploc container to create a compost. These can be found at most grocery stores.

Students should use local soil obtained from their own gardens. This is something that they would have been exposed to and experienced during the lessons in the STC Soils kit.

You will want to order worms for composting in advance of the creation of the compost. You can go to a local supplier. Here are some sites I found that also provide worms for composting.

http://www.topline-worms.com/

http://www.wormwrld.com/

All other materials should be the students' responsibility. However, if they are having trouble obtaining any material, feel free to give assistance.

This Webquest should last about 10 days to two weeks (45-minute to 1-hour class periods). Included in this is time not actually working on the Webquest, but time for students to gather the materials from home that they need to create their compost.

Credits:

I'd like to thank Kathryn Schotta for her work in preparing worksheets to be used in this Webquest and allowing me to adapt them to fit my needs.

Graphics and clipart used in the Webquest have been borrowed from the following sites:

http://www.marketwizz.com/backgrounds/

http://www.webclipart.about.com/od/animalsoriginal/1/blanim9.htm

http://www3.bc.sympatico.ca/hikersden/rules.html

http://www.clipartinc.com

http://www.pixelwiz.net

http://www.lbm.net/Clipart_Gallery/insects.htm

http://www.office.microsoft.com/clipart

THE NARRATIVE CURRICULUM

The narrative curriculum has the following assumptions:

- Stories are the way we make meaning of our lives.
- Stories are good tools for remembering things.
- Stories allow for learning in a meaningful context.
- Everyone can connect to stories.
- Stories provide a sense of community because of the universal human elements within them.
- Stories promote a constructivist approach.
- Authentic student inquiry emerges from stories.
- The KDB can be embedded in a story curriculum.
- Curriculum can be negotiated.
- The disciplines will be embedded in the stories and in the questions emerging from the stories, but they are not the organizing center.
- Narrative curriculum is marked by its recursiveness. Learners return again and again to the story to connect their explorations to it.

Lauritzen and Jaeger (1997) created a narrative curriculum that begins with a story or storylike context. Figure 7.8 offers a planning template of the narrative curriculum. Stories are selected to interest learners as well as to spark wonder. They are often stories with a science base. There is an interactive reading of the text, and student listening, questioning, and hypothesizing are encouraged. The teacher and students select questions to explore that can be investigated from a variety of disciplinary perspectives. The questions are organized so that they are under the umbrella of Big Questions. Aided by teacher input, students brainstorm how they can answer these questions. Students then commit themselves to answering a specific question.

Explorations are a key feature of narrative curriculum. They are open-ended routes that teachers develop with students to help them meet the challenge of an inquiry. The teacher does not have to know all the answers. Rather, the teacher gathers resources and materials and facilitates the students' learning. Specific standards are chosen for goals that are active in the curriculum. These standards direct the nature of the explorations and the culminations. They also inform the nature of assessment, which can occur both in the process of the explorations and culminations and in the products the students create. Assessments are often conducted through scoring guides or rubrics, some of which are custom made for the specific standard and some of which are preexisting (such as the inquiry or six-trait writing scoring guides). Student self-assessment and peer assessment are encouraged whenever possible either in addition to or alongside teacher-directed assessment. All assessment should inform instructional decisions regarding further needs to address the standards.

Disciplines are used as a heuristic in this approach. The students use the tools of the discipline that are needed; they act as scientists, historians, artists, or authors as dictated by the question asked. The culminations of these explorations are the communications students make with others in the learning community. Culminations can involve such tasks as demonstrations, dramatic re-creations, speeches, written work, and presentations of experimental results. The form of the culmination should be related to the investigations and specific standards. For example, if writing were a chosen goal, then a written product assessed with a scoring guide would be an expected part of the culmination. The audience of the culmination could be the community of learners in the classroom or be extended to a larger school audience or even into the greater community. In a project in which the students evaluated the recreational opportunities for children in their town, the audience was not only their classroom but also the city council. Regardless of the extent of the community of learners, the shared findings of all contribute to the context and thereby inform and transform the story.

What are the key features of the narrative curriculum? The narrative curriculum model is learner centered and allows for a variety of routes to knowing. The curriculum begins and ends in story. Reading the story aloud in a collaborative manner invites the children to bring their own life experiences, their personal stories, to an interaction with the original story. The children's responses—their puzzles, their wonderments, their desire to know—lead to explorations of new aspects that add to the children's life

Figure 7.8 The Narrative Curriculum Planning Template

Goals: Interpret human experience through literature and the arts. Think creatively and imaginatively when framing problems and seeking solutions. Social Science—Describe an issue from multiple points of view. Science—Use interrelated processes to pose questions and investigate the world.

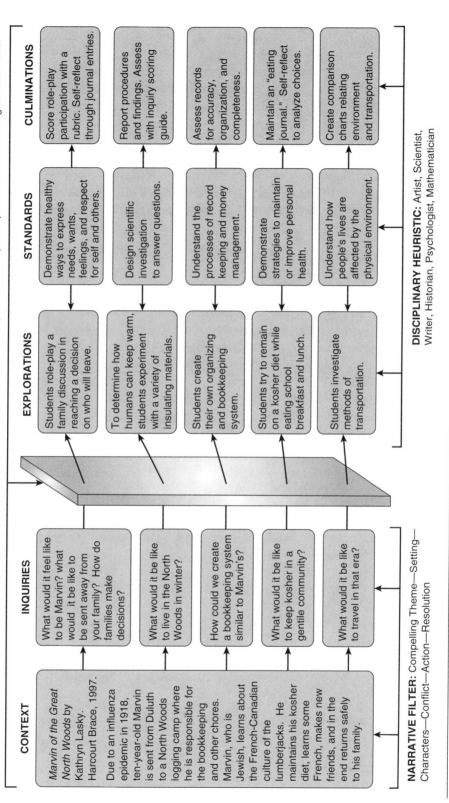

SOURCE: Carol Lauritzen and Michael Jaeger (2005).

stories. Students are encouraged to make connections between their own lives and the story. The rereading of the story, with all the new experiences intertwined, creates a new version of the text.

In the narrative curriculum design, the story is more than an anticipatory set to introduce areas of study. It is more than a springboard to launch children into inquiry. It is also a context that both invites and surrounds learning and gives meaning to all the children's investigations and explorations. Not only are stories long remembered, but also the learning that is generated from and intertwined with them is long remembered. The purpose of the narrative is to encourage student questioning. Their authentic desire to know becomes the focus of study. What they learn is blended with what they already know to construct new meaning.

CREATING AN INTERDISCIPLINARY COURSE WITH INTERDISCIPLINARY GUIDELINES

In February 2005, a new program was introduced at A.Y. Jackson Secondary School in Toronto. The program is called jPod. jPod is a facilitated, self-directed learning program based on appreciative inquiry. It features democratic decision making, individual timelines, and a student-run Code of Care Recommendation Committee. Students receive support in reaching particular learning goals. A central component is a vibrant, diverse community of learners who respect the principles of mutual respect and understanding. Students are guided toward meeting the curriculum expectations (standards) for the particular credit they are pursuing.

jPod is grounded in an appreciative inquiry approach. *Appreciative inquiry* is an intentional process of asking positive questions (Watkins & Mohr, 2001). It creates positive energy in the group and is an alignment of strengths to make the weaknesses irrelevant. Appreciative inquiry brings the best of the past forward, while creating a new vision for the future with the 4-D technique:

1. *Discover* the "best of what is"—identify where the school's processes work perfectly.

2. *Dream* "what might be"—envision processes that would work perfectly all the time.

3. *Design* "what should be"—define and prioritize elements of perfect processes.

4. Create a *destiny* based on "what will be"—participate in the creation of the design.

Students in jPod can obtain credits in any course currently existing within the Ontario Ministry of Education's (1999) document *Choices Into*

Action: Guidance and Career Education Program Policy for Ontario Elementary and Secondary Schools available at www.edu.gov.on.ca/eng/document/curricul/secondary/choicee.pdf. Students may also obtain interdisciplinary credits that can be used toward the six credits needed for entrance into postsecondary education. Students may wish to design their own unique interdisciplinary or locally developed courses that meet their interests and abilities. These courses are subject to the approval of the principal or board of education and ministry of education. During the personal admission interview, students specify which credits they are interested in, and the jPod staff determine if their selection can be accommodated on a case-by-case basis.

The expectations for teachers are as follows:

- To interview and select appropriate candidates for participation
- To identify the students' learning styles and facilitate accordingly
- To provide and suggest learning resources
- To empower and inspire participants to seek out their own learning resources
- To assess achievement on an ongoing basis through weekly discussion, cooperative group seminars, or observations (for example, an observation checklist)
- To acknowledge attendance and make prior arrangements for attendance options
- To conduct summative evaluations to allow students to demonstrate learning

The expectations for students are as follows:

- To work toward being self-directed and responsible learners
- To be respectful members of a learning community (e.g., timelines, healthy boundaries)
- To abide by the Code of Care and the Toronto District School Board and A.Y. Jackson codes of behavior
- To follow attendance guidelines
- To meet overall expectations of their courses as prescribed in the Ontario curriculum with assistance from the teacher
- To design and follow through on their learning plans
- To create their own student-created assessment pieces using Bloom's Taxonomy for foundation

Saeid's Story

Saeid Chavoshi is a Grade 12 student at A.Y. Jackson in the jPod program. He has designed his own Grade 12 credit course based on the

Ontario Curriculum Grades 11 and 12 Interdisciplinary Studies guideline (http://www.edu.gov.on.ca). This illuminating example describes an interdisciplinary credit course that is based on interdisciplinary standards as well as some standards within the disciplines. In addition, it illustrates how students can design and implement their own standards-based courses complete with appropriate evaluations.

Saeid has an avid interest in the mind. He is curious about self-awareness and meditation, character and personality, the mind's capabilities and how to enhance them, memory and efficient learning and memorization techniques, and the physical well-being of the brain. He designed his own course to study the mind and named it "Brain Science." His own words follow:

> I saw an opportunity to pursue my interest in Brain Science and to also gain a school credit for it. I started drafting ideas for units and resources to be organized in a systematic way so they could be taught at school through jPod. With the adamant support of a jPod teacher, Karen Leckie, the vice principal Alison Kelsey, and the principal Nancy Nightingale, I set out to write my own course profile. I read some of the ministry documents such as *The Ontario Curriculum, Grades 11 and 12: Interdisciplinary Studies, 2002* and *The Ontario Curriculum: Grade 11 and 12 Social Sciences and Humanities 2000*. [Both are available at http://www.edu.gov.on.ca.] I created a list of standards (expectations) for the course that included standards from interdisciplinary studies and from several of the social sciences and the humanities. I used some of the already existing interdisciplinary courses available on www.curriculum.org as a guide. See http://www.curriculum.org/occ/profiles/11/inter disciplinary.shtml as an example. I also used the Internet to find resources.
>
> To create the course, the overall standards for an interdisciplinary course must be covered, but how this is done is up to the student. Teachers are always present for assistance, and the amount and depth of formal instruction may vary depending on the need as established by the student and teacher. Evaluation is based on Student Created Assessment Pieces (SCAPs). The student submits a proposal containing a list of SCAPs and how they will address the standards outlined for their course. The students create original work related to their study and develop a rubric for evaluation. Every SCAP is followed by a teacher-student conference, and the teacher and student negotiate a mark.
>
> After getting the approval from the principal, I started the course with another student, Charles Xie, in the jPod program. We asked teachers who had the necessary interests and skills to help us. We are doing Units 1, 2, and 4 at the same time, dedicating a

certain amount of days per week for each unit. We spend two days on Unit 1, one day on Unit 2, and two days on Unit 4. This approach is working well. Currently, as part of this course, we practice yoga and kundalini meditation. Two teachers from jPod guide us in the yoga and mediation. We practice yoga two mornings per week with one teacher, and we meditate two mornings a week with the other teacher. With the help of the teachers, we have created a "meditation room" in our school that is open to all staff and students. The evaluation is based on the suggested activities and SCAPs (evaluations) outlined in each unit. The course itself is evolving every day, with more resources being added and more opportunities to apply our new knowledge in everyday life.

Brain Science: A Sample Interdisciplinary Studies Course

Brain Science

Social Science, Grade 12, Open Policy Document: The Ontario Curriculum, Grades 11 and 12: Interdisciplinary Studies, 2002 http://www.edu.gov.on.ca/eng/document/curricul/secondary/grade1112/inter/inter.html

Prerequisite: any university or university/college preparation course

Course Description

This course will help students develop and consolidate the skills required for and knowledge of different subjects and disciplines to solve problems, make decisions, create personal meaning, and present findings beyond the scope of a single subject or discipline. Students will apply the principles and processes of inquiry and research to use a range of print, electronic, and mass-media resources effectively. They will also assess their own cognitive and affective strategies, apply general skills in both familiar and new contexts, create innovative products, and communicate new knowledge.

This course provides a pragmatic approach to studying the mind, how it is influenced, and ways to enhance and improve its functions. Great emphasis will be placed on practical ways to use that knowledge in one's life. Skills learned from this course influence every aspect of the individual's life from school study to work and social relations. Major fields of study in this course include:

- The impact of society on the mind's perception
- Psychological influences on the brain's perception and thinking abilities
- Emotional influences on the mind's perception
- Ways to enhance and improve memory

- Efficient learning techniques
- Ways to increase reading speed and also improve comprehension
- The physical well-being of the brain
- Focus and ways of improving perception
- The history and practical use of meditation

The course profile is divided into five units as delineated in Figure 7.9.

Figure 7.9   Units for Brain Science

Unit 1	Mind's Perception	20 hours	15%
Unit 2	Physical Well-Being of the Brain	10 hours	10%
Unit 3	Improving the Capabilities of the Mind	30 hours	20%
Unit 4	Meditation and Self-Awareness	35 hours	25%
Unit 5	Culminating Performance Task	15 hours	30%

SOURCE: Saeid Chavoshi.

A Sample Unit

Unit 1: Mind's Perception

Time: 20 hours

This unit will explore the many influences society has on our judgments, perceptions, and prejudices. The function and perception abilities of the mind are profoundly influenced by the individual's mood and emotions, which in turn are ramifications of physical well-being and social interactions. In this unit, students will learn to recognize some of those influences to alleviate some of their negative impacts.

Broad-Based Interdisciplinary Standards

Theory and Foundation

- Demonstrate an understanding of the key ideas and issues related to each of the subjects or disciplines studied
- Demonstrate an understanding of the different structures and organization of each of the subjects or disciplines studied
- Demonstrate an understanding of the different perspectives and approaches used in each of the subjects or disciplines studied

Processes and Methods of Research

- Be able to plan for research, using a variety of strategies and technologies
- Be able to assess and extend their research skills to present their findings and solve problems

Implementation, Evaluation, Impacts, and Consequences

- Implement and communicate information about interdisciplinary endeavors, using a variety of methods and strategies

Standards were also included from the following subjects:

HIR3C—Managing Personal and Family Resources Grade 11 College Prep

HIP3E—Managing Personal Resources Grade 11 Workplace Prep

HPC30—Parenting Grade 11 Open

HHS4M—Individual and Families in a Diverse Society Grade 12 University/College Prep

HHG4M—Issues in Human Growth and Development Grade 12 U/C Prep

HSP3M—Introduction to Anthropology, Psychology, Sociology Grade 11 U/C Prep

Activities and Evaluations

1. Students write a journal reflecting on what they learned from reading each book on the resources list. Students need to include personal feedback.

2. Students read *Constructing a Life Philosophy.* Choose one viewpoint to reflect on, and write a written report on these reflections.

3. From one of the resources, students will take a key lifestyle idea (i.e., don't make assumptions) and through an oral presentation, show how they have been able to implement it in their lives and what effects it had. If the person wasn't able to implement a key lifestyle idea, he or she will explain why. Was the idea too abstract or unrealistic, or did social conditions preclude it?

4. Each student will choose a viewpoint from the book *Constructing a Life Philosophy.* Give an oral presentation to explain what it is, how it relates to our society today, if it is realistic or logical, and why. Discuss if and how the viewpoint is biased.

5. To end the unit, each student will find another media resource that contains germane information regarding the influences on the mind's perception and share it through both an oral presentation and a written report.

Resources

Kielburger, C., & Kielburger, M. (2004). *Me to we: Turning self-help on its head.* Etobicoke, Canada: John Wiley & Sons.

Kornfield, J. (2000). *After the ecstasy, the laundry: How the heart grows wise on the spiritual path.* New York: Bantam.

Ruiz, D. (1997). *The four agreements: A practical guide to personal freedom.* San Raphael, CA: Amber Allen.

Schmidt, M. (1993). *Constructing a life philosophy.* San Diego, CA: Greenhaven.

This chapter outlined a variety of ways that educators are making meaning of standards-based curriculum. They show that it is possible to create a relevant curriculum and also to create a rigorous one that meets the required standards. In the next chapter, we will follow consultant Tessie Torres-Dickson and her schools in Florida to see how standards-based integrated curriculum can be implemented successfully.

DISCUSSION QUESTIONS

1. Compare and contrast the different models offered in this chapter.

2. What model appeals to you or could be most effective in your own context?

3. How do these models achieve alignment of the curriculum?

4. How does the process of curriculum design in these models compare to the backward design process?

5. Curry and Samara design generic assessment tools. The generic assessment tool can be used regardless of subject area every time a student performs a specific skill. Figure 7.4 is one example—in this case, it is a generic tool for a timeline. Curry and Samara have created many others for specific grade levels for things such as pie charts, friendly letters, demonstrations, and class discussion (see www.curriculumproject.com). What are the advantages of such templates? disadvantages?

6. Review the KDB Umbrella in Figure 1.4. This umbrella fits Saeid Chavoshi's unit on "Brain Science: A Sample Interdisciplinary Studies Course." How could you use the notion of interdisciplinary standards as a guide? What do you think the interdisciplinary standards should be?

SUGGESTED ACTIVITIES

1. Choose a Big Skill (e.g., communication) or a subskill of a Big Skill (e.g., presentation, mock interview, newscast, oral book report, poem, poster, tree chart). Create a generic assessment tool for it. Look at the model in Figure 7.4.

2. On the Internet, use the keyword *Webquest* on Google. This will bring you to many resources on making a Webquest (for example, http://webquest.org/). Find a relevant Webquest and critique this Webquest. Is the curriculum aligned? How well does it follow the principles in this book? How could you use it?

3. Choose one of the models offered and create your own curriculum using the same standards as you did for previous activities.

8

A Journey From Beginning to End

Designing and Implementing the Curriculum Process Model

Tessie Torres-Dickson

National Educational Consultant

http://www.tessiedickson.com

For the past three years, I was fortunate enough to work closely with several magnet schools throughout the country. I acted as a facilitator for designing interdisciplinary standards-based curriculum. I used the Curriculum Process Model™. I created this model based on 25 years of educational experience working with teachers on interdisciplinary approaches.

Let's begin with a visit to three extraordinary magnet schools in the Pinellas School District located near St. Petersburg, Florida. The first stop is Maximo MicroSociety Elementary. On Main Street, students are conducting business at the school's local bank and post office. Further down, students are conducting a trial, with an actual judge, lawyers, and jury. In this microsociety, the students elected Maximo's town mayor in a schoolwide election. In the fifth-grade classrooms, students are actively engaged in learning about the three branches of government; they use their wireless laptops to conduct research on the Internet and prepare for their PowerPoint presentations using an LCD projector.

The next stop is Gulfport Montessori Elementary. A challenge for many Montessori schools is how to teach the Montessori curriculum while meeting the state standards. Some Montessori schools attempt to overcome this dilemma by "matching" rather than "aligning" their curriculum with the state standards. At Gulfport Elementary, teachers have successfully aligned their curriculum with the state standards and still teach to the high demands of an interdisciplinary Montessori curriculum.

Our final destination is Campbell Park Marine Science Elementary. An enormous black-and-white whale's tail emerges from the ground to welcome visitors. The whale symbolizes the theme of "marine science." Brilliant marine-life wall paintings are exhibited throughout the school grounds. In the marine science lab, various science investigations are scattered throughout the room. Excited students examine and handle marine science organisms in the touch tank. Entering a classroom, students are occupied with a manatee Webquest. This is an inquiry Web-based research project focusing on questions students have about manatees. Their task is to write a detailed factual letter to the governor of Florida to convince him that he should try to help save the Florida manatee.

Continuing on to the primary classrooms, students are involved in water conservation projects. They are conducting inquiry-based science investigations about water. In another classroom, the students are dissecting a real shark to learn about its structures and functions and to understand how it is able to survive in the open oceans. Outside, students are conducting science investigations as they collect data from the grass marsh they planted earlier in the year.

This visit to the magnet schools reveals active and engaging learning environments. Students are involved in various rigorous and relevant learning experiences as they construct their own knowledge through real-life community issues. In all three schools, grade-level teachers collaboratively plan and design their comprehensive curriculum. The schools all successfully designed a schoolwide standards-based interdisciplinary curriculum for the entire school year. Also, they delivered the mandates of their particular magnet school. How have these schools been able to accomplish this challenging and enormous task?

The remainder of this chapter describes the journey that these schools experienced while implementing the Curriculum Process Model. Although I would love to write about each of the schools and their success stories, I am using Campbell Park Marine Science Magnet School's story to illustrate the process. Here, educators have designed and implemented schoolwide standards-based interdisciplinary curriculum since 2002. This chapter focuses on the work of Sharlene Annie Lee, Barbara

Johnson, and Judi Watkins, who developed a 13-week unit. The curriculum is in Appendix C. The Florida standards (Florida Education Standards Commission, 2000) were used throughout the process.

THE CURRICULUM PROCESS MODEL

Planning and implementing a schoolwide standards-based interdisciplinary curriculum is a complex and ongoing process. It could never happen without the key players first having the vision and then providing ongoing support and adequate time for educators to plan. Figure 8.1 describes the four phases involved in this process.

Phase 1

Phase 1 involved a series of meetings with the magnet project director, administrators, magnet curriculum coordinators, and teachers to determine the needs of the school. Goals were identified for Campbell Park Marine Science Magnet School. The school committed itself to long-term professional development. The participants understood that this commitment was essential to the success of this process. Professional development began with a full-day orientation that involved all the educators in the school, including the administrators. The orientation helped educators to understand the rationale for a standards-based interdisciplinary curriculum and their own roles in successfully establishing a K–12 spiral curriculum.

Before Campbell Park began its long-term professional development, the school had encountered many dilemmas. The educators were faced with the overwhelming task of implementing an exemplary marine science curriculum while incorporating the state standards for all disciplines. To add to the confusion, the school also had other school initiatives it was responsible for implementing. Teachers pondered the dilemma of how they were going to infuse all the school's initiatives into the curriculum without losing the integrity of each initiative.

Texts or other instructional materials had driven the school's marine science magnet curriculum. The result was a fragmented curriculum with instructional gaps that hit or missed the state standards. As teachers followed the textbooks, they found themselves matching the curriculum to the standards. This is much less effective than aligning the standards to the curriculum. As a result, many teachers became frustrated and overwhelmed. Aligning standards to classroom practices is an extremely complex process. It takes time, patience, and leadership. The alignment of curriculum, assessment, and instruction, however, is vital to success in improving instruction.

As the facilitator of the professional development, I focused largely on a fundamental principle of the Curriculum Process Model—a backward

Figure 8.1   Standards-Based Interdisciplinary Curriculum Process Model

Standards-Based Interdisciplinary Curriculum Process Model			
Phase	**Action Plan**	**Timeline**	**Outcome/Product**
Phase 1	1. Meet with Administrators and Curriculum Coordinators to determine and discuss curriculum goals.	Before beginning the Process Model, then monthly and ongoing throughout the years.	1. Administrators support a Standards-Based Curriculum. 2. Goals and outcome assessment.
	2. Educators participate in orientation and various workshops on Standards-Based Curriculum.	First day of Professional Development, then ongoing throughout the year.	Educators understand their role in a K–12 spiral curriculum.
Phase 2	1. Educators meet in grade-level teams to design yearlong Standards-Based Interdisciplinary Units, and engage in the Process Model focusing on Curriculum, Assessment, and Instruction.	Beginning of the Process Model, then ongoing throughout the years.	1. Professional Learning Community 2. Standards-Based Interdisciplinary Conceptual Units
	2. Unpack and cluster the State Standards and Benchmarks for science and social studies, then unpack and cluster all other disciplines.	Beginning of the Process Model and throughout the year. Make changes when necessary.	1. Curriculum Alignment 2. Vertical/Horizontal Charts indicating State Standards and Benchmarks taught in each discipline/units and grade.
	3. Grade-level teams design a Yearlong Conceptual Map illustrating concepts and topics aligned to the State Standards & Benchmarks to be taught year-round.	Beginning of the Process Model and throughout the year. Make changes when necessary.	1. Connects units and concepts throughout the year. 2. Yearlong Conceptual Map for each grade level. 3. Post in classroom.
	4. Conduct cross-grade-level collaboration to discuss Curriculum, Assessment, and Instruction.	After all State Standards and Benchmarks are mapped, and throughout the year.	Promotes cross-grade-level collaboration, ensures a spiral curriculum, avoids gaps in the curriculum, and builds a schoolwide Professional Learning Community.

Standards-Based Interdisciplinary Curriculum Process Model			
Phase	**Action Plan**	**Timeline**	**Outcome/Product**
Phase 2 Cont'd	5. Determine Formative and Culminating Assessments for units, with emphasis on incorporating authentic assessments.	Beginning of planning stages, and before determining and selecting learning experiences.	1. Targets teaching and learning 2. Promotes Authentic Assessments.
	6. Educators develop and select rigorous and relevant learning experiences aligned to the State Standards and Benchmarks.	Ongoing process.	1. Real-world and meaningful learning situations. 2. Promotes project-based learning experiences.
	7. Create Timeline for each unit, depicting where concepts, essential questions, and projects will be incorporated throughout the unit.	After completing the planning for each unit.	Provides a guide for teaching and learning, and connects all grade-level classrooms.
	8. Construct "Standards-Based Curriculum Binders," to replace traditional lesson plan books.	After completing the stages of the Standards-Based Curriculum planning template.	1. Living Document. 2. Standards-Based Curriculum Unit Binders for each grade-level team.
Phase 3	1. Implement the Standards-Based Interdisciplinary Curriculum designed in each grade level.	Beginning of Year Two, and ongoing.	Implementation of a K–12 spiral curriculum.
	2. Document where State Standards & Benchmarks have been taught and assessed for each discipline, and for each unit.	During implementation of units and throughout the years.	1. Collection of data. 2. Taught and Assessed Standards & Benchmarks Chart.
	3. Continue building capacity by implementing, revising, monitoring, and evaluating the curriculum.	Throughout the years.	1. Living document: revisions, modifications, and evaluations to yearlong units. 2. Builds capacity.
Phase 4	1. Model teaching opportunities, and continuous grade-level and cross-grade-level meetings.	Ongoing	1. Promotes professional growth. 2. Educators learn various teaching strategies and integration methods.

(Continued)

Figure 8.1 (Continued)

Standards-Based Interdisciplinary Curriculum Process Model			
Phase	**Action Plan**	**Timeline**	**Outcome/Product**
Phase 4 Cont'd	2. Educators receive coaching visits by Consultant, Curriculum Coordinators, and Administrators.	Throughout the years, and during classroom observations.	Educators receive support for implementation of the interdisciplinary units.
	3. Educators attend workshops to enhance the curriculum and present their work to other educators.	Ongoing	1. Professional growth. 2. Promotes best practices.
	4. Sustain curriculum through continuous planning, implementing, revising, monitoring, and evaluating the Standards-Based Interdisciplinary Curriculum.	Ongoing	1. Builds capacity. 2. Improves student achievement. 3. Promotes systemic change.

SOURCE: Tessie Torres-Dickson.

planning approach. Teachers started planning with the state standards, rather than with the textbook or activities. The primary goal of Campbell Park was to have teachers teach the standards through a marine science perspective.

Phase 2

In Phase 2 of the Curriculum Process Model, teachers worked collaboratively in grade-level teams. This phase is extremely effective if conducted with one grade-level team at a time. It ensures adequate time for powerful discussions as teachers begin to unpack and cluster the state standards. The teachers used a standard-based, interdisciplinary conceptual unit planning template to identify standards and establish the goals of a unit, align authentic assessments, and develop instructional learning experiences to promote student achievement. The teachers used the Florida standards (Florida Education Standards Commission, 2000).

The grade-level teams began the process by scanning their science and social studies state standards. They identified keywords in the science and social studies standards to determine big interdisciplinary concepts and understandings. For example, the third-grade team chose to study the concepts of conservation, interdependence, adaptation, and communication.

While the teams scanned the standards, they simultaneously constructed a yearlong conceptual map. This was a graphic organizer that illustrated the interdisciplinary concepts and topics to be taught throughout the year. The map also showed how one unit builds on another, interconnecting all the unit concepts throughout the year.

This stage was extremely complex. As a facilitator, I continually asked inquiry-type questions to guide the teachers through the process. The concepts and topics included on the yearlong map must clearly be aligned to the standards across the disciplines. Figure 8.2 shows two of the three interconnected units of the third grade's yearlong conceptual map. Each grade-level team constructed a yearlong conceptual map for their year. The maps were displayed in each classroom all year offering a visual representation of the school's yearlong units of study. The significance of these maps lies in the fact that each map is strategically constructed to build on each grade level's units, ensuring and promoting a K–5 spiral curriculum.

Next, the grade-level teams identified the standards and benchmarks they needed to teach for each unit. They developed a vertical and horizontal chart for each discipline to indicate when standards and benchmarks were taught throughout the year. Figure 8.3 presents an example of a small section of a science K–2 vertical/horizontal chart. Figure 8.4 offers a small sample of a science Grades 3 to 5 vertical/horizontal chart. These charts provide valuable information for identifying where the gaps are (if any) in teaching the state standards from kindergarten through fifth grade.

The charts also triggered schoolwide discussions about how the standards were being taught during multi-grade-level collaborations. Administrators used these charts to evaluate their school's progress and ensure the spiraling in a K–5 curriculum. This stage built a professional learning community and promoted a schoolwide collaboration among all educators.

At this point, grade-level teams generated interdisciplinary Essential Questions to guide the unit. Essential Questions are significant in the Curriculum Process Model because they drive the planning of assessment and instruction and the careful selection of learning experiences. Again, this was a facilitated process. The Essential Questions were aligned to the standards and focused on the higher levels of Bloom's Taxonomy. They centered on major issues, problems, or concerns that were relevant to students' lives, communities, and world. These questions required students to connect learning from several disciplines and to make personal connections. Teachers also generated concept and topic questions that focused on the specific concepts and topic of study.

Now they are ready to determine what is most important to understand, do, and be. A look at the Grade 3 unit "Lean on Me" helps show how all these pieces fit together (Appendix C). Sharlene Annie Lee, Barbara Johnson, and Judi Watkins used the unit planning template to create a 13-week unit. Once they completed Phase 1, they could identify the Understand/Do/Be. The Understand/Do/Be chart is in Appendix C.

166

Figure 8.2   Two Units of the Third-Grade Yearlong Conceptual Map

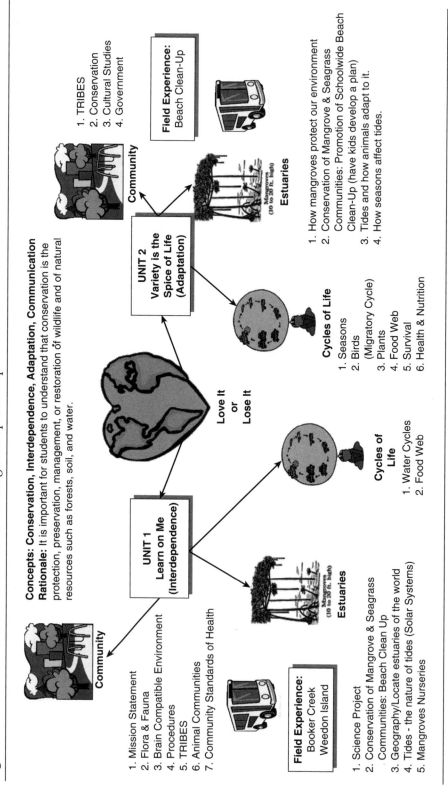

Concepts: Conservation, Interdependence, Adaptation, Communication

Rationale: It is important for students to understand that conservation is the protection, preservation, management, or restoration of wildlife and of natural resources such as forests, soil, and water.

Love It or Lose It

UNIT 1
Learn on Me
(Interdependence)

Community

1. Mission Statement
2. Flora & Fauna
3. Brain Compatible Environment
4. Procedures
5. TRIBES
6. Animal Communities
7. Community Standards of Health

Field Experience:
Booker Creek
Weedon Island

1. Science Project
2. Conservation of Mangrove & Seagrass Communities: Beach Clean Up
3. Geography/Locate estuaries of the world
4. Tides - the nature of tides (Solar Systems)
5. Mangroves Nurseries

Estuaries

Mangroves
(10 to 20 ft. high)

Cycles of Life

1. Water Cycles
2. Food Web

UNIT 2
Variety is the Spice of Life
(Adaptation)

Community

1. TRIBES
2. Conservation
3. Cultural Studies
4. Government

Field Experience:
Beach Clean-Up

Estuaries

Mangroves
(10 to 20 ft. high)

1. How mangroves protect our environment
2. Conservation of Mangrove & Seagrass Communities: Promotion of Schoolwide Beach Clean-Up (have kids develop a plan)
3. Tides and how animals adapt to it.
4. How seasons affect tides.

Cycles of Life

1. Seasons
2. Birds (Migratory Cycle)
3. Plants
4. Food Web
5. Survival
6. Health & Nutrition

SOURCE: Sharlene Annie Lee, Barbara J. Johnson, and Judi Watkins.

Figure 8.3   Campbell Park Science Grades K–2 Vertical/Horizontal Chart

Campbell Park Elementary School Science Yearlong Units Grades K–2 Vertical/Horizontal Chart		Unit 1: Similarities & Differences	Unit 2: Relationships	Unit 3: Responsibilities	Unit 1: As the Tides Turn	Unit 2: Affects in Our Lives	Unit 3: Conservation-One Life to Live	Unit 1: Adaptation	Unit 2: Growth & Development	Unit 3: Cause & Effect
		Kindergarten			First Grade			Second Grade		
Strand A: The Nature of Matter										
Standard 1: The student understands that all matter has observable, measurable properties.										
SC.A.1.1.1	Knows that objects can be described, classified, and compared by their composition (e.g., wood or metal) and their physical properties (e.g., color, size, and shape)	X	X		X	X		X	X	X
SC.A.1.1.2	Recognizes that the same material can exist in different states.		X		X	X			X	X
SC.A.1.1.3	Verifies that things can be done to materials to change some of their physical properties (e.g., cutting, heating, and freezing), but not all materials respond the same way (e.g., heating causes water to boil and sugar to melt).		X		X	X				X
Standard 2:	The student understands the basic principles of atomic theory.									
SC.A.2.1 .1	Recognizes that many things are made of smaller pieces, different amounts, and various shapes.	X	X		X	X		X	X	X

SOURCE: Tessie Torres-Dickson.

NOTE: X Indicates benchmarks taught in each unit for each grade level

Figure 8.4   Campbell Park Science Grades 3–5 Vertical/Horizontal Chart

Campbell Park Elementary School Science Yearlong Units Grades 3–5 Vertical/Horizontal Chart		Unit 1: Lean on Me	Unit 2: Variety Is the Spice of Life	Unit 3: Can You Hear Me Now?	Unit 1: Are You Digging It	Unit 2: Stop the Presses!	Unit 3: To Infinity and Beyond!	Unit 1: Circles of Life	Unit 2: Patterns of Change	Unit 3: The World From Where I Stand
		Third Grade			Fourth Grade			Fifth Grade		
Strand A: The Nature of Matter										
Standard 1: The student understands that all matter has observable, measurable properties.										
SC.A.1.2.1	Determines that the properties of materials (e.g., density and volume) can be compared and measured (e.g., using rulers, balances, and thermometers). AA-MC	X	X	X	X		X		X	X
SC.A.1.2.2	Knows that common materials (e.g., water) can be changed from one state to another by heating and cooling. CS-MC		X	X	X		X		X	X
SC.A.1.2.3	Knows that the weight of an object always equals the sum of its parts. CS-MC			X			X		X	
SC.A.1.2.4	Knows that different materials are made by physically combining substances and that different objects can be made by combining different materials. AA-MC		X		X		X			X
SC.A.2.1.5	Knows that materials made by chemically combining two or more substances may have properties that differ from the original materials. CS-MC		X				X			X

SOURCE: Tessie Torres-Dickson.

NOTE: X Indicates benchmarks taught in each unit for each grade level

Phase 2 continued with grade-level teams designing or selecting interdisciplinary authentic assessments. Project-based and performance-based assessments were carefully determined before learning experiences were considered. Assessments were aligned to the state standards and directly linked to instruction. What was taught, was tested. As a result, the expectations for student performance were clear to both teachers and students. Formative assessments were used to evaluate students prior to and throughout the unit instruction. Summative and culminating assessments were designed to evaluate students' overall understanding at the end of the unit.

Once the assessments were determined, grade-level teams selected or created learning experiences. Choosing the activities last ensures curriculum alignment. During this stage, educators were encouraged to provide rigorous and relevant learning experiences. They adopted a constructivist teaching and learning philosophy. Instructional activities were set in the real world as much as possible.

Throughout the process, I provide a number of templates to guide educators in their planning. Figure 8.5 shows the standards-based, interdisciplinary lesson plan form that establishes consistency and contains crucial aspects for a standards-based interdisciplinary curriculum.

A learning experience chart indicated how the learning experiences incorporated Bloom's taxonomy, the multiple intelligences, interdisciplinary connections, and the identification of the standards and benchmarks taught. The learning experience chart revolves around each essential question (see Figure 8.6).

The planning process completed, grade-level teams created an instructional timeline. This visual tool provided a method for organizing the teaching and learning, and it was helpful to map each week's activities. It was a vital part of the curriculum binders. It also encouraged cohesiveness among grade-level teachers and classrooms during implementation.

Phase 2 concluded with the construction of a standards-based curriculum binder for each unit. The curriculum binders replaced the traditional teacher lesson plan books, and they were distributed to incoming educators with expectations to utilize and implement the yearlong units. This avoided any loss of instructional time, especially for first-year teachers. The curriculum binders provided consistency within the grade levels but still allowed for freedom and creativity in effectively implementing the curriculum. The administrators used their copy to monitor and evaluate the curriculum implementation. The binder contained the following components:

- Standards-based yearlong conceptual map
- Standards-based unit instructional timeline
- Standards-based unit planning template
- Daily and weekly lesson plans with rigorous and relevant learning experiences

Figure 8.5   Lesson Plan Form

Standards-Based Interdisciplinary Lesson Plan Form	
Unit Title:	
School:	
Grade Level:	
Duration:	
Description of Lesson:	(Clearly describe what the students are expected to do. Background knowledge may be included in this section.)
State Standards and Benchmarks:	(Include the standards and benchmarks from all disciplines that apply to this lesson.)
Interdisciplinary Essential Question(s):	(Which Unit Essential Questions will be addressed?)
Interdisciplinary Assessments:	(Describe the method of assessment, and which standards and benchmarks are specifically being assessed.)

Rigorous & Relevant Learning Experiences:	
Materials:	(Describe how the lesson will be taught.) (Make a list of the materials needed.)
Preparations:	(Clearly describe the steps to prepare for the lesson.)
Procedures:	(Include a step-by-step process to teach the lesson.)
Resources/Web sites:	(Include a list of resources/Web sites that may be used.)
Instructional Strategies:	(Include a variety of teaching and learning strategies.)
Differentiated Instruction:	(Include the differentiated instruction that will meet the variety of learning needs for students.)
Bloom's Taxonomy:	(Include a variety of levels, making sure the higher levels are targeted.)
Multiple Intelligences:	(Include a variety of learning styles to meet individual needs.)

SOURCE: Tessie Torres-Dickson.

172

Figure 8.6   Standards-Based Interdisciplinary Conceptual Unit Planning Instructional Learning Experiences

Standards-Based Interdisciplinary Conceptual Unit Planning
Instructional Learning Experiences

Name of Unit: _____   **Marking Period Unit Will Be Taught:** _____

Interdisciplinary Essential Questions:

Learning Experiences engaging students in exploring the Essential Questions	Assessment	Bloom's Taxonomy Level(s)	Multiple Intelligences	Goal 3 Standards	Science	Social Studies	Language Arts	Mathematics	Foreign Language	Health, Music, Art, & P.E.	Technology

SOURCE: Tessie Torres-Dickson.

- Standards-based interdisciplinary learning experiences chart
- K–5 vertical charts for all disciplines
- State Standards and Benchmarks Taught and Assessed chart
- Teaching and learning resources

Phase 3

The focus in Phase 3 was the implementation of the yearlong units. Grade-level teams continued to meet to develop and revise their yearlong units. These units became "living documents" reflecting the latest research developments and best practices. The Standards and Benchmarks Taught and Assessed Chart provided a collection of data for ensuring that the standards and benchmarks were being taught and assessed (Figure 8.7).

Phase 4

The Standards-Based Curriculum Process Model concluded with Phase 4. This phase included opportunities for ongoing professional growth for educators as they implemented their standards-based curriculum. Observing model teaching of standards-based interdisciplinary lessons, onsite coaching, and mentoring were beneficial during this phase. Emphasis was placed on sustaining the curriculum through continuous planning, implementing, revising, monitoring, and evaluating the curriculum.

SOME INSIGHTS

Designing and planning units using the standards-based curriculum model is an effective approach to maintaining the identified standards as the focus of the instruction and assessment. Working through the planning process helped the unit developers to be precise in selecting and designing instructional activities and led to better student performance.

Teaching to standards and teaching for understanding is generally more time consuming than traditional teaching. Moving from traditional subject-specific teaching to a standards-based curriculum needs to be done gradually.

Professional development focusing on collaboration offers an opportunity for sustainable systemic change in a school. As educators work closely together to design curriculum, they develop a professional learning community in their grade-level teams. These communities further evolve into a schoolwide professional learning community as educators engage in cross-grade-level team discussions focusing on the curriculum, assessment, and instruction.

These magnet schools experienced the Curriculum Process Model through a long-term professional development. They successfully developed and created a professional collaborative culture in their schools, where all educators were united in their commitment to student success.

Figure 8.7   Taught and Assessed Standards and Benchmarks (Standards-Based Interdisciplinary Conceptual Units. Science 3–5)

Standards-Based Interdisciplinary Conceptual Units Science 3–5: Taught & Assessed Standards & Benchmarks
School:
Strand A: The Nature of Matter
Standard 1: The student understands that all matter has observable, measurable properties.
1. Determines that the properties of materials (e.g., density and volume) can be compared and measured (e.g., using rulers, balances, and thermometers). **AA-MC**
Unit One: Taught & Assessed
Unit Two: Taught & Assessed
Unit Three: Taught & Assessed
Unit Four: Taught & Assessed
2. Knows that common materials (e.g., water) can be changed from one state to another by heating and cooling. CS-MC
Unit One: Taught & Assessed
Unit Two: Taught & Assessed
Unit Three: Taught & Assessed

SOURCE: Tessie Torres-Dickson.

For the past three years, the magnet schools worked diligently on designing their standards-based interdisciplinary conceptual units. Their efforts continue. Phase 4 is not really the end. Rather, it is a new beginning for these educators, who are unquestionably enjoying the journey.

TESSIE TORRES-DICKSON'S ACKNOWLEDGMENTS

This chapter is dedicated to the memory of Earl Manheimer, who was an inspiring teacher who never gave up the concept of planning and teaching through a standards-based interdisciplinary curriculum. After 30 years of teaching at Campbell Park Elementary, sadly, Earl passed away, after his recent retirement from the Pinellas School District.

This chapter is also dedicated to all the inspiring and devoted educators at the following schools:

Pinellas School District—Florida

Campbell Park Marine Science Elementary—James Steen

Congratulations to the third-grade teachers for receiving the 2005 Magnet Schools of America Merit Award, in designing their yearlong standards-based interdisciplinary units (Sharlene Lee, Barbara Johnson, Tina Reuter, Judi Watkins)

Gulfport Montessori Elementary—Lisa Grant

Maximo MicroSociety Elementary—Dr. Barbara Hires and Sandra O'Bryant

Lansing Public Schools—Michigan

Centre for Language, Culture, and Communication Arts Middle School—LaDonna Mask

Woodcreek Math, Science & Technology Elementary—Rita Cheek

Pleasant View Visual & Performing Arts Elementary—Madeline Shanahan

Riddle Visual & Performing Arts Middle School—Edna Robinson

A special thanks to Dr. Charlene Einsel, Elaine Ranieri, and Worsie Gregory, three dynamic women who have given me the opportunity to work with their districts and who have believed in me from the beginning. And an immense thanks to Susan Drake, who has given me the opportunity to write a chapter about the schools' successful experiences. And a very special thank-you to my supporting and loving husband Johnny, who has been extremely patient and has given me the courage and strength to believe that I, too, can make a difference and have an impact on education.

DISCUSSION QUESTIONS

1. What is similar in the three schools described at the beginning of the chapter?

2. Review the steps that Tessie outlines for the standards-based interdisciplinary Curriculum Process Model. Why are there so many steps? Is there anything that might be added? Omitted?

3. Figure 8.2 shows a part of the yearlong conceptual map. The teachers created this map with Inspiration software. How would this type of mapping process work in your situation?

4. These teachers completed a Scan and Cluster using the forms such as those found in Figure 8.3 and Figure 8.4. Could you create charts such as these to guide your Scan and Cluster in your context?

5. Tessie has developed an Understand/Do/Be framework that is very similar to the Know/Do/Be that is offered in this book. Which term do you prefer? Why?

6. Critique the "Lean on Me" unit for its alignment.

7. In Figure 8.5, Tessie offers a template for ensuring relevant and rigorous learning experiences. Figure 8.6 allows the curriculum designers to check that they have done this. She includes resources, instructional strategies, differentiated instruction, Bloom's taxonomy, and multiple intelligences. How effective have the authors of "Lean on Me" been in including all these elements?

8. As Tessie has indicated, there are many elements that can and perhaps should be included in designing an integrated curriculum that is both relevant and rigorous. In your opinion, which elements *must* be included?

SUGGESTED ACTIVITIES

1. After you have decided on the most important elements necessary for a rigorous and relevant curriculum, review and revise your own curriculum to include these elements.

2. Using Figure 8.1, plan for the implementation of your interdisciplinary curriculum in your local context.

Epilogue

As I come to the end of this book, I find once more that it is never really the end. I carefully make final edits to address reviewers' concerns, and I discover new ideas and new examples. I am eager to add more—include this or that. My own understanding deepens. But I must stop.

Long ago, I discovered that neither researching about nor teaching an integrated curriculum could be done using a zoom lens only. Interdisciplinary curriculum needs to be set in the Big Picture of education—considering aspects such as leadership, educational change, educational reform, pedagogy, philosophy, constructivism, accountability, and evaluation and assessment. And as the Big Picture changes, as it inevitably does, so must one's understanding of how to integrate the curriculum.

Chapter 8 of this book offers a wonderful example of the many aspects that one must consider to implement such an approach throughout a school. Tessie Torres-Dickson shares her step-by-step process to guide educators through the complexity of the process. She shows that both accountability and relevance can be achieved.

The teachers in this book are also a living testimony that integrated approaches can be implemented in a culture of accountability. Where there is a will, there is a way. Their stories speak for themselves. The fact that you as a reader have come to the last paragraph on the last page also speaks for itself. Like me, I am sure that you will discover that this particular adventure never ends and continues to open new doors and bring fascinating new insights. Welcome.

DISCUSSION QUESTION

Now that you have read this book and engaged in discussion and activities, discuss what you would write in your own epilogue.

Appendix A:
A Standards-Based
Curriculum Unit

Saga of Survival: An integrated unit of study involving science, math, and English for a Grade 10 academic class modified from the work of Will Lammers and Laura Tonin.

1. Broad-based curriculum standards (www.edu.gov.on.ca) selected after a horizontal and vertical Scan and Cluster:
   - Solve problems involving quadratic functions. (Math)
   - Solve problems involving the analytic geometry concepts involving lines. (Math)
   - Solve trigonometric problems involving right or acute triangles. (Math)
   - Use a variety of organizational techniques to present ideas and information logically and coherently in written work. (English)
   - Sort and label information, ideas, and data; evaluate the accuracy, ambiguity, relevance, and completeness of the information, and draw conclusions based on the research. (English)
   - Produce written work for a variety of purposes, with the purpose of analyzing information, ideas, themes, and issues and supporting opinions with convincing evidence. (English)
   - Spell specific academic and technical terms correctly. (English)
   - Examine the factors that affect the survival and equilibrium of populations in an ecosystem, including heat transfer in weather systems. (Science)

- Examine how abiotic (nonliving) factors affect the survival and geographic location of biotic (living) communities, and investigate the effects of heat transfer on development of weather systems. (Science)
- Plan and conduct research into ecological relationships. (Science)

2. Web identifying potential clusters of standards and content:

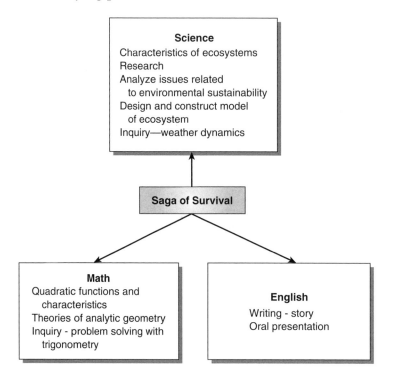

Science
Characteristics of ecosystems
Research
Analyze issues related
  to environmental sustainability
Design and construct model
  of ecosystem
Inquiry—weather dynamics

Saga of Survival

Math
Quadratic functions and
  characteristics
Theories of analytic geometry
Inquiry - problem solving with
  trigonometry

English
Writing - story
Oral presentation

3. Classification of learning outcomes in a Know/Do/Be Umbrella:

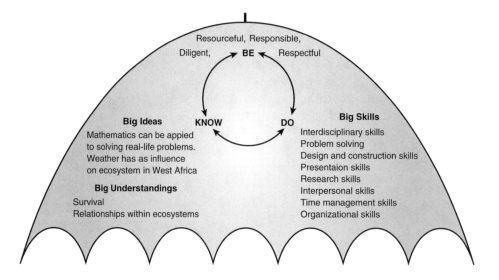

Resourceful, Responsible,
Diligent,   **BE**   Respectful

KNOW   **DO**

Big Ideas
Mathematics can be appied
to solving real-life problems.
Weather has as influence
on ecosystem in West Africa

Big Understandings
Survival
Relationships within ecosystems

Big Skills
Interdisciplinary skills
Problem solving
Design and construction skills
Presentaion skills
Research skills
Interpersonal skills
Time management skills
Organizational skills

4. Big Assessment task:

Polly, an avid traveler and sailor, fell into a predicament and has survived to tell about it. Last year, during a transworld solo sailing expedition, her sailboat sank during a storm. She managed to survive the disaster by swimming to the nearby island of Kwa Dratique, which is located in the tropics off the coast of West Africa. She has an incredible story to tell about her experiences, but it is sketchy. She is able to narrate to you the saga of her survival in general terms, but specifics are lacking.

You and a partner have been given the task of documenting Polly's story. You will be presenting her story as part of a community fair to commemorate her homecoming. A number of stands will be set up at the fair. Small groups of people from the community will visit you at your stand.

Your presentation of Polly's story should show the *process* you followed, as well as the *product* you created, as described in the following:

a. To fill in the details of Polly's story, your presentation should account for the following *processes:*
    - Show all of your research work in a learning log. Each entry should be dated.
    - Solve one of Polly's problems using trigonometry.
    - Solve one of Polly's problems using quadratic functions.
    - Solve one of Polly's problems using analytic geometry of line segments.
    - Show evidence of how Polly rationalized her food consumption, based on her environment and her resources.
    - Show how the weather systems on Kwa Dratique affected where and how she lived, given the geography of the land and its climate.

b. You should be prepared to present the following *products:*
    - Create an oral presentation of Polly's story.
    - Create a stand-alone display outlining the details of your story.
    - Organize information in two or more different ways (e.g., charts, graphs, text).
    - Document the references you used on your display.
    - Create a model that represents a typical ecosystem on Kwa Dratique.
    - Answer any questions for visitors, or provide any clarifying information.

SAGA OF SURVIVAL

Rubric for Assessment of Project and Display

Names of presenters:

Criteria	Level 1 (Below expectations)	Level 2 (Barely meets expectations)	Level 3 (Meets expectations)	Level 4 (Exceeds expectations)
(/point total)	(points per level)			
Display: Creativity (/5)	Display does not catch the reader's interest. (2)	A small portion of the display catches the reader's attention. (3)	Most of the display catches the reader's attention. (4)	The whole display catches the reader's attention. (5)
Layout (/5)	Display is difficult to follow, **and** it has a sloppy appearance. (Lettering is unclear or illegible, and illustrations are not clearly presented.) (1–2)	Display is difficult to follow, **or** it has sloppy a appearance. (3)	Display is easy to follow, and it has a generally neat appearance. (4)	Display is easy to follow, has an excellent overall appearance, and makes good use of space allowed. (5)
Content (/5)	Display lacks information, **and** content is not self-explanatory. (0–1)	Display lacks information, **or** content is not self-explanatory. (2–3)	Display contains all relevant information and is self-explanatory. (4)	Displayed information is detailed, relevant, and self-explanatory. (5)
Learning log: Content (/5)	Entries are not titled or dated, log is an incomplete record of work done, **and** references are not documented. (0–1)	Entries are not titled or dated, **or** log is an incomplete record of work done, **or** references are not documented. (2–3)	Entries are titled and dated, log is a complete record of work done, and sources are referenced. (4)	Log contains all required content, and there is evidence of self-reflection as project progressed. (5)

Criteria	Level 1 (Below expectations)	Level 2 (Barely meets expectations)	Level 3 (Meets expectations)	Level 4 (Exceeds expectations)
(/point total)	(points per level)			
Organization (/5)	Notebook lacks —names, date, and title on cover; —signs of being well used; **and** —neatness and legibility. (0–1)	Notebook lacks **2 of** —names, date, and title on cover; —signs of being well used; —neatness and legibility. (2–3)	Notebook lacks **1 of** —names, date, and title on cover; —signs of being well used; **or** —neatness and legibility. (4)	Notebook shows —names, date, and title on cover; —signs of being well used; —neatness and legibility. (5)
Story: Inventiveness and mechanics of writing (/5)	The story lacks a coherent plot. (1)	The plot is coherent, but it is difficult to follow or not realistic. (2–3)	The plot is coherent and realistic. (4)	The plot is coherent, is realistic, and contains an element of surprise.
Story: Grammar and spelling conventions (/5)	Writing contains more than five spelling and grammar errors. (0–2)	Writing contains three to five spelling and grammar errors. (3)	Writing contains not more than two spelling and grammar errors. (4)	Writing is free of spelling and grammar errors. (5)
Integration of content (/5)	Two (2) or more processes or products are missing from story. (0–2)	One (1) process or product is missing from story. (3)	All required elements of content are evident in story. (4)	All required elements of content are evident, and there is evidence of more analysis than expected. (5)
Use of terminology, units of measurement (/5)	Three (3) or more terms and units of measurement are either missing or used incorrectly. (0–2)	Two (2) terms and units of measurement are either missing or used incorrectly. (3)	One term or unit of measurement is either missing or used incorrectly. (4)	All terms and units of measurement are included and used correctly. (5)
Interpretation of data (/5)	There is little or no evidence that measurements and calculations were used to add meaning to the story. (0–2)	There is some evidence that measurements and calculations are used to add meaning to the story. (3)	Most measurements and calculations are used to add meaning to the story. (4)	Every measurement and calculation is used to add meaning to the story. (5)
Total:				50

5. Big Questions

What difficulties did Polly face, and what resources did she need to survive?
How do natural forces affect survival?
How can mathematics be used to solve real-life problems?

6. Instructional activities and assessments
   a. Standards reclustered according to mini-units.

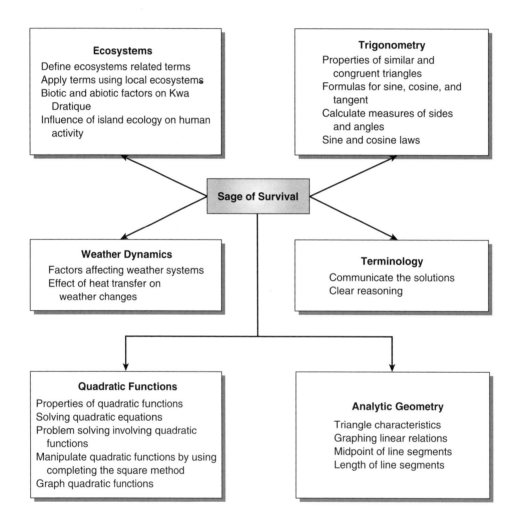

b. Sample Mini-Unit: Ecosystems

Teaching/Learning Experience	Standard	Assessment
In groups, students brainstorm for roles that different people in a community need to play for the community to be self-sufficient. Teacher assigns each small group a role identified in the community. Small groups research using text or media-based resources to determine the name and description of the part of the ecosystem that plays a role similar to that identified in the community. Teacher shows visual display of Kwa Dratique and poses the following question: If you were to recommend that Polly reside in a particular location on the island, where would you locate her, and why? There are no roads on Kwa Dratique, and Polly must rely on the ecology of the land to survive.	Examine the factors (natural and external) that affect the survival and equilibrium of populations in an ecosystem. (Science) Investigate potential topics by formulating questions. (English) Examine how abiotic factors affect the survival and geographical location of biotic communities. (Science) Use a variety of organizational techniques to present ideas logically and coherently in written work. (English) Use the formula of length of a line segment to solve problems. (Math) Use the formula of midpoint of a line segment to solve problems. (Math) Focus on interpreting and analyzing information, ideas, themes, and issues and supporting opinions with convincing evidence. (English)	Each group shares its ideas, and teacher notes them on board for display. Teacher evaluates ideas for completeness. Teacher distributes a research rubric prior to activity. Students negotiate standards. Peer evaluation using rubric. Students generate a research- and problem-solving-skills rubric. Teacher collects and evaluates individual work.

SOURCE: Adapted from the work of Will Lammers and Laura Tonin.

RESOURCES

Drake, S. M., & Burns, R. (2004). *Meeting standards through integrated curriculum.* Alexandria, VA: ASCD.

Ontario Ministry of Education and Training. (1999). *The Ontario curriculum. Grades 9 and 10 English.* Toronto, Canada: Author.

Ontario Ministry of Education and Training. (1999). *The Ontario curriculum. Grades 9 and 10 mathematics.* Toronto, Canada: Author.

Ontario Ministry of Education and Training. (1999). *The Ontario curriculum. Grades 9 and 10 science.* Toronto, Canada: Author.

Appendix B: A Rubric and Reflection Tool to Use as a Guide for Creating Your Own Standards-Based Interdisciplinary Curriculum

	Level 1	Level 2	Level 3	Level 4
Scan and Cluster	There has been no attempt to scan and cluster.	Horizontal and vertical scans are not complete and do not lead to meaningful clusters or do not address the meta-level.	Horizontal or vertical scan was done well and addresses the meta-level in most cases.	Both horizontal and vertical scans are thorough and include meaningful clusters of standards that work at the meta-level.
Selection of Broad-Based Standards	Broad-based standards are not chosen thoughtfully.	Broad-based standards act as an umbrella for the meaningful clusters in a hit-or-miss fashion.	In most cases, broad-based standards act as an umbrella for meaningful clusters.	Broad-based standards act as an umbrella for meaningful clusters.
Construction of Web	No evidence to show the cluster was done using the standards.	Standards are not clustered in a coherent way.	Standards are clustered coherently, with minor omissions.	All standards are clustered coherently.
Topic or Theme Choice	Illogical choice of topic with regard to scan and cluster.	Topic is not age appropriate or interesting to students.	Topic is age appropriate or interesting to students.	Topic is age appropriate or interesting to students and is backed up with informally collected student feedback.
Construction of Know/Do/Be (KBD) Umbrella	Incomplete.	KDB elements (Big Understandings/Big Ideas, Big Skills) are confused.	KDB elements clearly described.	Elements are concisely described, and the *be* is insightfully linked to the *know* and the *do*.
Description of Big Assessment Task	Minimal description of the task.	Description of the task but with few	Clear description of the task with many	Clear description of the task with many

Task-Specific Rubric	Rubric created with imprecise language and lacking meaningful and relevant indicators.	Rubric created with imprecise language and some meaningful and relevant indicators. connections to the KDB Umbrella.	Rubric created in precise language with meaningful and relevant indicators in both teacher and student versions. connections to the KDB Umbrella.	Rubric created with explicit, meaningful, and relevant indicators in precise language in both teacher and student versions. substantive connections to the KDB Umbrella.
Creating Big Questions	Questions are simplistic and require a single answer.	Includes topic and questions that could be more focused; questions tend to be simplistic, with few opportunities for multiple answers.	Includes topic and Big Questions; questions encourage inquiry and multiple answers.	High level of relevance of Big Questions and topic questions; questions encourage inquiry and use multiple answers as the focus of reflection.
Unit Relevance	Questions deal with a few parts of the unit.	Questions deal with individual parts of the unit.	Questions deal with substantial parts of the unit and reflect student input.	Questions reflect student input and have a high degree of relatedness to the unit.

QUESTIONS FOR REFLECTION

Big Assessment Task

- Does the assessment provide a way to celebrate learning?
- Does the assessment provide an external audience to witness or assess the performance or demonstration?

Daily Activities and Assessments

- Keeping the connection to the KDB Umbrella in mind, how do the daily activities align with the Big Assessment task?
- Choose two activities or assessments and discuss how you will know when the student has learned them.
- Have you used any traditional assessments? Why or why not?
- If you used traditional assessments, describe the connections you made in format and skill level to the standardized testing students will be required to complete.
- Describe your first assessment and discuss the reasons for the choices you made, given what you know about assessment.
- Describe your second assessment and discuss the reasons for the choices you made, given what you know about assessment.
- What would you describe as your most significant learning from this process?

SOURCE: A rubric and reflection tool to use as a guide for creating your own standards-based interdisciplinary curriculum. From the work of Glynnis Fleming (glynnis.flemming@dsbn.edu.on.ca).

Appendix C: Lean on Me (A Sample Curriculum Using the Curriculum Process Model

STAGE 1: CURRICULUM

1. *Step 1.* Establish the Big Idea concepts that will be the focus for this unit.
   - Conservation, Interdependence, Change

2. *Step 2.* Determine the purpose and desired outcomes as a result of this unit.
   - Students will understand the concept of interdependence in the classroom and in the coastal environment. We will study the relationship and interaction between plants, animals, and humans, including the element of human impact. The desired outcomes will be for students to demonstrate responsibility and care for the environment and to be collaborative and productive citizens in the community.

3. *Step 3.* Identify and cluster the targeted standards and benchmarks that will drive the teaching and learning for this unit.
   - Focus on science or social studies standards and benchmarks. (Refer back to Figures 8.3 and 8.4.)

AUTHOR'S NOTE: This unit is based on the work of Sharlene Annie Lee, Barbara J. Johnson, and Judi Watkins.

4. *Step 4.* Generate interdisciplinary essential questions to guide the unit.
   - How do plants and animals depend on each other to survive?
   - How do the basic structures and functions of plants and animals affect their survival?
   - How do members of a community live together and share or compete for resources?
   - How does the cyclical nature of our environment impact coastal communities (e.g., moon, weather)?
   - What kinds of impacts do humans make on the environment, and how do they affect our future?

5. *Step 5.* Generate topic questions that focus on the specific area of study.
   - How do the members of our school community depend on each other?
   - Why is it important to work together in a community?
   - Do you think Weedon Island is a wilderness free of humans? Why or why not?
   - How are mangroves and seagrass affected by the environment?
   - Why is the water cycle important?

6. *Step 6.* What standards and benchmarks from other disciplines will be integrated in this unit?
   - The teachers integrated relevant standards using the vertical and horizontal charts for language arts, mathematics, health, foreign languages, and technology.

Figure C.1   Understand/Do/Be Framework

Understand/Do/Be Framework		
Interdisciplinary Concepts: What concepts will students Understand?	Complex Interdisciplinary Performance Skills: What will students be able to Do?	Student Character: How will students Be different?
All organisms depend on each other for survival.	Illustrate the dynamic relationship in a food web and distinguish between the changing roles in the web (prey and predator).	Be conscientious and take responsibility for their role in not disrupting the food web.
The impact of human activities on the environment.	Compare and contrast positive and negative human impact on the environment.	Be responsible, protect and respect the environment.
The essential components of a community.	Experience and discuss components of a community.	Be collaborative and helpful in the community.
There are predictable, repeatable, definable cycles in nature.	Predict environmental effects due to the cycles in nature (e.g., moon and tides, weather and seasons)	Be critical thinkers.

SOURCE: Tessie Torres-Dickson. tessiedickson@earthlink.net; (863) 660-5700.

7. *Step 7*. What are the interdisciplinary conceptual understandings, performance skills, and character traits that students will acquire during the unit?
   - Figure C.1 shows the Understand/Do/Be framework.

STAGE 2: ASSESSMENT

8. *Step 8*. How will student progress be monitored throughout the unit?
   - Role play (developer, home builder, environmentalist, etc.).
   - Chart data collected on human impact.
   - Create a storyboard on a nature cycle (art, song, drama).
   - Use a concept map or graphic organizers to chart positive or negative community life. Write reports, a research project, or recommendations based on research.
   - Construct a food web using yarn.
   - Use notes or journals from study trips.
   - Keep a journal of questions to be answered throughout the unit.
   - Have a teacher-generated test that includes: multiple choice, short response, and extended response, which reflect the benchmarks tested on the Florida Comprehensive Assessment Test.
   - Use the rubric as a guide.

9. *Step 9*. What is your culminating assessment?
   - Booker Creek project: Your group will investigate one of the Essential Questions using your research skills. Keep a list of your own questions as you proceed. Pick a specific area and observe seasonal changes over time (examples: birds, real-time creek data, field trip). Your group will create a presentation of your research (traditional, iMovie, HyperStudio, PowerPoint). A rubric will be used for evaluation.

STAGE 3: INSTRUCTION

10. *Step 10*. What rigorous and relevant learning experiences are there?

    1. *How will you capture students' interest to kick off this unit?*
       - "Being there" experiences, including outdoor learning at Booker Creek and study trips to Weedon Island.

    2. *What rigorous and relevant learning experiences will engage students in learning? Which activities will be used for formative assessment?*
       - Draw a Scientist
       - Scavenger Hunt for Field Guide Book
       - Booker Creek Photo ID Field Guide (asssessment)

- Graphing Our Weather (compare to another area in the country) (assessment)
- Designing a Habitat
- Weedon Island Field Trip (assessment)
- Marsh Munchers
- Are You Me?
- Hit or Miss
- Water Cycle Activities
- Service Project: Coastal Clean-Up
- Digit Delight
- PowerPoint Projects (asssessment)
- Algebra Patterning
- Kidspiration Graphic Organizers (asssessment)
- Estuaries Around the United States and the World
- Tide Activities and Graphing Local Tide Information (assessment)
- Mangroves/Nursery/Food Webs/Crabs

3. *What performance-based or project-based learning experiences will be implemented in this unit?*
   - Booker Creek investigations, which include various projects such as PowerPoint, posters, and field guides.
   - Coastal Clean-Up in Pinellas County beaches.
   - PowerPoint presentations.

4. *What instructional strategies will be incorporated to teach the concepts?*
   - Small cooperative groups (Students work together with designated roles.)
   - Brainstorming (Students contribute ideas related to a topic.)
   - Teacher modeling (Teacher models activities such as Power Point, note taking, etc.)
   - Know/Want to Know/How Learned Chart
   - Graphic organizer (Students will use various visual aids to collect data.)
   - Problem solving (Students will work together in cooperative groups to problem solve various learning experiences.)
   - Field experience: Being there (A planned learning experience for students to observe, study, and participate in a setting off the school grounds.)
   - The learning cycle (Students explore the concept, behavior, or skill with hands-on experience.)
   - Reflective thinking (Students reflect on what was learned after a lesson is finished.)
   - Free writing (Students respond in writing for a brief time to a prompt, a quote, or a question.)

- Think, pair, share (Students reflect on a topic and then pair up to discuss, review, and revise their ideas.)
- Venn diagrams (Students list unique characteristics of two items or concepts representing the similarities and differences.)
- Predicting, observing, explaining (Students predict, observe, and explain various findings during investigations.)
- Learning logs (Students will record daily observations and data in their science journals.)

5. *How will you differentiate learning to meet the needs of all students?*
   - Activities will be modified to meet individual needs.

References

Aikin, W. M. (1942). *The story of the eight-year study.* New York: Harper.

Albright, S., & Breidenstein, A. (2004). A school with a worldview. *Eutopia Online.* Retrieved November 16, 2005, from www.glef.org

Allen, R. (2005). Cyber sources. *Curriculum Technology Quarterly, 14*(3), D.

Beane, J. (1993). *A middle school curriculum: From rhetoric to reality.* Columbus, OH: National Middle School Association.

Beane, J. (1997). *Curriculum integration: Designing the core of democratic education.* New York: Teachers College Press.

Billig, S. (2000). *The impacts of service learning on youth, schools and communities: Research on K–12 school-based service learning, 1990–1999.* Denver, CO: RMC Research Corp. Retrieved April 20, 2005, from http://www.learningindeed.org/research/slresearch/slrsrchsy.html

Black, P., Harrison, C., Lee, C., Marshall, B., & Wiliam, D. (2003). *Assessment for learning.* Berkshire, UK: Open University Press.

Brown, D. F. (2006). It's the curriculum, stupid: There's something wrong with it. *Phi Delta Kappan, 87*(10), 777–783.

Carnegie Corporation. (1989). *Turning points: Preparing youth for the 21st century.* New York: Carnegie Corporation of New York.

Commonwealth of Pennsylvania Department of Education. (2005). *The Pennsylvania code: PA code 1.8.* Retrieved November 16, 2005, from http://www.pde.state.pa.us/k12/lib/k12/Reading.pdf

Conference Board of Canada. (1992). *Employability skills profile: What are employers looking for?* (Brochure E-F). Ottawa, Canada: Author.

Connell, R. (2003). *Research and evaluation into the Curry/Samara Model® of curriculum, instruction and assessment.* Houston, TX: Aldine Independent School District, and Austin, TX: The Curriculum Project.

Curry, J., Samara, J., & Connell, R. (2005). *The Curry/Samara Model®: Curriculum, instruction and assessment yield statistically significant results.* Retrieved November 16, 2005, from http://www.curriculumproject.com

Curtis, D. (2003). We're here to raise kids. *Eutopia Online.* Retrieved November 16, 2005, from www.glef.org

Darling-Hammond, L. (2004). Standards, accountability, and school reform. *Teachers College Record, 106*(6), 1047–1085.

Darling-Hammond, L., & Falk, B. (1997). Using standards and assessments to support student learning. *Phi Delta Kappan, 79*(3), 1990–1999.

Drake, S. M. (1991). How our team dissolved the boundaries. *Educational Leadership, 49*(2), 20–22.

Drake, S. M. (1993). *Planning for integrated curriculum: The call to adventure.* Alexandria, VA: Association for Supervision and Curriculum Development.

Drake, S. M. (1998). *Creating integrated curriculum: Proven ways to increase student learning.* Thousand Oaks, CA: Corwin Press.

Drake, S. M., & Burns, R. (2004). *Meeting standards through integrated curriculum.* Alexandria, VA: Association for Supervision and Curriculum Development.

Earl, L. (2003). *Assessment as learning.* Thousand Oaks, CA: Corwin Press.

Elmore, R. F., & Rothman, R. (1999). *Testing, teaching and learning: A guide for states and school districts.* Washington, DC: National Academy Press.

Erickson, H. L. (2001). *Stirring the head, heart, and soul: Redefining curriculum and instruction* (2nd ed.). Thousand Oaks, CA: Corwin Press.

Expeditionary Learning Outward Bound. (2001). *Evidence of success.* Retrieved November 16, 2005, from http://www.elob.org/publications/evidence.pdf

Expeditionary Learning Outward Bound. (2003). *Expeditionary learning core practice benchmarks.* Garrison, NY: Author.

Ferrero, D. J. (2006). Having it all. *Educational Leadership, 63*(8), 8–14.

Florida Education Standards Commission. (2000). *Subject matters content standards for Florida's teachers.* Retrieved November 16, 2005, from http://www.firn.edu/doe/dpe/publications/contentstandards03.pdf

Fogarty, R. (1991). *The mindful school: How to integrate the curricula.* Pallantine, IL: Skylight.

Foley, A. & Condon, M. (2005, April). Taking back ownership of curriculum standards. Paper presented at ASCD Conference, Orlando, FL.

Hargreaves, A. (2003). *Teaching in the knowledge society.* New York: Teachers College Press.

Hargreaves, A., & Earl, L. (1990). *Rights of passage.* Toronto, Canada: Queen's Printer.

Henderson, C. (2000). Vertical teams yield vertical achievement in southeastern Texas school district. *Education in Practice, 9,* 9–12.

Jacobs, H. H. (Ed.). (1989). *Interdisciplinary curriculum: Design and implementation.* Alexandria, VA: Association of Supervision and Curriculum Development.

Jacobs, H. H. (Ed.). (1997). *Mapping the big picture: Integrating curriculum and assessment.* Alexandria, VA: Association of Supervision and Curriculum Development.

Jacobs, H. H. (Ed.). (2004). *Getting results with curriculum mapping.* Alexandria, VA: Association of Supervision and Curriculum Development.

Jensen, E. (2005). *Teaching with the brain in mind.* Alexandria, VA: Association of Supervision and Curriculum Development.

Kee, E. (2005). Multimedia *Macbeth*: Web project fosters deeper understanding of the human condition. *Curriculum Technology Quarterly, 14*(3), 4–6.

Kielburger, C., & Kielburger, M. (2004). *Me to we: Turning self-help on its head.* Etobicoke, Canada: John Wiley and Sons.

King, K. V., & Zucker, S. (2005). *Curriculum narrowing.* Retrieved November 16, 2005, from http://harcourtassessment.com/hai/Images/pdf/assessmentReports/CurriculumNarrowing.pdf

Kornfield, J. (2000). *After the ecstasy, the laundry: How the heart grows wise on the spiritual path.* New York: Bantam.

Kovalik, S. (1994). *ITI: The model-integrated thematic structure* (3rd ed.). Kent, WA: Books for Educators.

Lachowicz, J. (2004). Curriculum mapping in alternative education settings. In H. H. Jacobs (Ed.), *Getting results with curriculum mapping* (pp. 97–111). Alexandria, VA: Association for Supervision and Curriculum Development.

Lauritzen, C., & Jaeger, M. (1997). *Integrating learning through story: The narrative curriculum.* Albany, NY: Delmar.

Littky, D. (2004). *The big picture.* Alexandria, VA: Association for Supervision and Development.

Manzo, R. K. (1996). Districts pare electives for core courses. *Education Week.* Retrieved April 20, 2005, from http://www.edweek.org/ew/articles/1996/12/11stand.h16.html

Miller, L. (2004, September). Mapping the journey to school success. *Professionally Speaking*, 51–56.

Mitchell, F. M. (1998). *The effects of curriculum alignment on mathematics achievement of third grade students as measured by the Iowa Test of Basic Skills: Implications for educational administration.* Unpublished dissertation, Clark Atlanta University, Atlanta, GA.

Ohio State Department of Education. (2001). *Office of regional school improvement services: A case study of key effective practices in Ohio's improved school districts.* Bloomington: Indiana Center for Evaluation, Smith Research.

Ontario Ministry of Education. (1999). *Choices into action: Guidance and career education program policy for Ontario elementary and secondary schools.* Toronto, Canada: Queen's Printer. Retrieved November 16, 2005, from http://www.edu.gov.on.ca/eng/document/curricul/secondary/choices/index.html

Ontario Ministry of Education. (2000). *The Ontario curriculum: Grade 11 and 12 social sciences and humanities.* Toronto, Canada: Queen's Printer. Retrieved November 16, 2005, from http://www.edu.gov.on.ca/eng/document/curricul/secondary/grade1112/inter/inter.html

Ontario Ministry of Education. (2002). *The Ontario curriculum grades 11 and 12 interdisciplinary studies.* Toronto, Canada: Queen's Printer. Retrieved November 16, 2005, from http://www.edu.gov.on.ca/eng/document/curricul/secondary/grade1112/inter/inter.html

Ontario Ministry of Education. (2003). *Think literacy: Cross-curricular approaches grade 7–12.* Toronto, Canada: Ontario Ministry of Education.

Ontario Ministry of Education. (2004). *The Ontario curriculum: Social studies 1–6 history and geography 7–8.* Toronto, Canada: Queen's Printer. Retrieved November 16, 2005, from http://www.edu.gov.on.ca/eng/document/curricul/ social/

Paulson, A. (2005, May 5). A classroom as big as the world. *Christian Science Monitor.* Retrieved November 16, 2005, from http://www.csmonitor.com/2005/0510/p11s02-legn.html?s+hns

Public Schools of North Carolina State Board of Education. (2003). *North Carolina standard course of study: Social studies.* Retrieved November 16, 2005, from http://www.ncpublicschools.org/curriculum/socialstudies/scos/2003–04/002philosophy

Ruiz, D. (1977). *The four agreements: A practical guide to personal freedom.* San Raphael, CA: Amber Allen.

Schmidt, M. R. (1993). *Constructing a life philosophy.* San Diego, CA: Greenhaven.

Schmied, K. (2005). *A view that matters: Understanding essential questions.* Allentown, PA: Performance Learning Systems, Inc.

Schmied, K. (2005, April). Did you ask a good question today? Paper presented at ASCD Conference, Orlando, FL.

Smith, C., & Myers, C. (2001). Students take center stage in classroom assessment. *Middle Ground, 5*(2), 10–16.

State of Vermont Department of Education. (2005). *Vermont's framework of standards and learning opportunities.* Retrieved November 16, 2005, from http://www .state.vt.us/educ/new/pdfdoc/pubs/framework.pdf

Stevenson, C., & Carr, J. (1993). *Dancing through walls.* New York: Teachers College Press.

Tomlinson, C., Kaplan, S. N., Renzulli, J. S., Purcell, J., Leppien, J., & Burns, D. (2002). *The parallel curriculum: A design to develop high potential and challenge high-ability learners.* Thousand Oaks, CA: Corwin Press.

Truesdale, V., Thompson, C., & Lucas, M. (2004). Use of curriculum mapping to build a learning community. In H. H. Jacobs (Ed.), *Getting results with curriculum mapping* (pp. 10–24). Alexandria, VA: Association for Supervision and Curriculum Development.

Udelhofen, S. (2005). *Keys to curriculum mapping.* Thousand Oaks, CA: Corwin Press.

U.S. Department of Labor, the Secretary's Commission on Achieving Necessary Skills. (1991). *What work requires of school: A SCANS report for America 2000.* Washington, DC: Author.

Vars, G. (2001). Editorial comment: On research, high stakes testing and core philosophy. *Core Teacher, 50*(1), 3.

Watkins, T. M., & Mohr, B. J. (2001). *Appreciative inquiry: Change at the speed of imagination.* San Francisco: Jossey-Bass.

Wiggins, G., & McTighe, J. (2005). *Understanding by design* (2nd ed.). Alexandria, VA: Association for Supervision and Curriculum Development.

York University. (2005). *York University.* Retrieved October 10, 2006, from http:// www.yorkuniversity.ca

Index